scribe-geezer

T H R E E   E S S A Y S

□ ○ ▷ ✿ △ ThePattern

b r e a k a w a y

LiTeRaCY

LifePlanning
by Floyd Wray

f l o y d   w r a y

Start Here

1. Tap the SETTINGS application on your phone/tablet.

2. Confirm that the camera is enabled to read QR-code.

3. In the SETTINGS application, also confirm that you're connected to the Internet. Return to home screen.

4. Tap the CAMERA icon to open the camera on your phone/tablet.

5. Aim the camera at the square QR-code box (above).

6. Click the permission screen that appears on the device screen. (Best practice: use widescreen orientation)

7. Set audio levels, pause, play, reverse, forward using the media-controller on your phone-tablet.

For trouble-shooting: https://vimeo.com/728287509

scribe-geezer

Floyd Wray

One who imagines animated visualizations
An old man

Motionbooks.com, LLC
Springfield, Missouri
65804

ISBN: 979-8-218-02884-8

Floyd Wray
SCRIBE-GEEZER
Published by: Motionbooks.com, LLC

Audio Effects licensed by The Hollywood Edge Sound Effects Library, The Premiere Edition

AI Voice Generation licensed by Blaster Suite/Speechelo. Additional vocal work created by the author

A CIP record for this book is available from the Library of Congress Cataloging-in-Publication Data

Distributed by Motionbooks.com, LLC
2733 East Battlefield Road, #217
Springfield, Missouri, 65804

For Spot & Dot

scribe-geezer
Table of Contents

ThePattern - Scribe   Page 7
1 The Nature of Reality   2 Uncle Morrie is Not A Pet
3 Narrative Patterns   4 Origins & Destiinies
5 Patterns of the Soul   6 What Do You Say To A Fish?
7 What Drives Cat Ownership?   8 My Fulturite - My Faith
9 Visible Light|Invisible Patterns   10 X-Event

Breakaway Literacy - Scribe   Page 40
1 Roach of the World   2 The Straight Line
3 Mouse Trauma   4 Authoring
5 Context Records   6 Crossing the Narrative Boundary
7 Scribing   8 Next Year's Words

LifePlanning - Scribe   Page 65
1 Scoping Out The Future   2 Is There A Higher Purpose?
3 What Did Your Ancestors Know   4 SANTAfication
5 Lands You Do Not Know   6 How Jesus Approached LifePlanning
7 Three Issues of Character   8 Expectation
9 Devil Dog   10 X-Event

LifePlanning Journal - Text   Page 90
1 Scoping Out the Future   2 Is There A Higher Purpose?
3 What Did Your Ancestors Know   4 SANTAfication
5 Lands You Do Not Know   6 How Jesus Approached LifePlanning
7 Three Issues of Character   8 Expectation
9 Devil Dog   10 X-Event

Appendices - Scribe   Page 196
1 Surviving the Rapture Scribe Test
2 Holybook Scribe Test

Floyd Wray

□ ○ ⬠ ✩ △ ThePattern

Preface to ThePattern

They're usually invisible to us, but they're everywhere: reoccurring themes in religion, history, science, art, and math.

Perhaps that's a bit misleading. Patterns are not actually invisible, they just tend to go unnoticed most of the time.

There's an old saying: *It's the thread that leads to the string, that leads to the rope, that leads to the chain.* This perfectly describes the way patterns work. The mathematics that originate in finger-counting during childhood, for example, may initiate a pattern-trail that leads to calculus and differential equations, later. Patterns, discovered in one concept, feed and grow within another. Oh, and the *string-to-the-rope* observation is also a pattern. The concept may be applied to mathematics, and practically any other discipline we undertake.

Patterns may actually be used to predict discovery. After graphing a sequence of sub-atomic particles, physicist Murray Gell-Mann discovered a hole in the visual symmetry. A missing piece. Based on the visualization, he started searching for an unknown particle. Two years later, he discovered the Omega-minus particle. Patterns reveal. Patterns predict. Patterns explain. Patterns can assist you in winning the Nobel Prize.

ThePattern / Scribing
The subject of patterns is perfectly suited to a narrative format that is–in itself–based on patterning.

Scribing designates a class of visual language that's been around since the beginning of time, or at least since humans started painting stories on cave walls. Scribing provides an illustration of a person, place or thing. It may also be the core component in visual analogy.

ThePattern employs animated visualizations to engage and inform.

ThePattern

1 The Nature of Reality

Not long ago I saw a bumper sticker that got me thinking about the nature of reality. Exactly how did you come up with your *snapshot* of the cosmos?

My fourth grade teacher, Ms. Stubbs, was a woman with a bizarre reality. She owned at least five-hundred cats, wore something purple every day, and when she taught us about Egypt, she pranced around the classroom channeling Queen Nefertiti. We were her *wee Nubians*, she said. Didn't have a clue what she was talking about. Her snapshot was more than a little creepy, but hey, it was hers to do with as she pleased.

Everyone has a sense-of-reality, filled with personal preferences and understanding. Like a fingerprint, it's unique. What interests me is how you come up with it. There are so many things in the universe, ready to lend shape to your inner landscape. Just how did your sense of the cosmos, form?

A few questions come to mind, immediately. Have you lent shape to your reality, or has your reality lent shape you? You can edit it, you know, throwing out the stupid stuff, but do you? And if you don't, why not?

Our reality holds: our likes, dislikes, our dumb ideas,

our smart ideas, our belief, our evidence, milestones, data-points, analogies, metaphors, and patterns-of-understanding, among other things. How in the world did all this stuff get into our heads?

On day one you were a blank-headed goo-ball of love; ten years later, you were an urbane, informed explorer of time and space. When you think about it, this represents a rather profound transition.

In the beginning, there were so many things you didn't know. Yet somehow, you reached out with a baby's hand, grabbed a small bit of the cosmos, and methodically, grew a mind with it. This was possible due to a simple little bit of magic: *you have an instinct for comparing things.* This is how your reality starts. Actually, this is how everything about you starts.

When you saw something, out there, you compared it to things you already knew, in here. Comparing patterns, evaluating the similarities and distinctions, led to increased understanding, and something else.

Patterns gave birth to more patterns, and in the process, you got smart. Intellectually, that's the difference between you at one, and you at ten. Thanks to patterning, comparing new things to known things, you transformed from a blank slate into a 10-year old genius.

10-year old
GENIUS

ThePattern

2 Uncle Morrie is Not A Pet

A pattern is a theme, an organizational theme. A pattern provides form and identity to objects and events. A pattern is a shared understanding; it suggests the nature of a thing.

Patterning is the *engine-of-intellect*. And while it's a personal transaction, one that's often invisible as a process, patterning is not just something we do, individually; patterning is also an inheritance from family and friends – from our community.

As an example, let's say, baby sees a hairy creature with four legs, that's not uncle Morrie, and mommy calls it a *dog*. Mommy's not afraid of the dog, so baby figures, even though it doesn't look like us, dogs must be OK.

Then baby sees a cat, and baby says, *dog*. Everyone laughs and mommy says, "No honey, that's a *cat*." Well, the cat doesn't look like a dog, now that you mention it, but mommy's not afraid of the cat either, so cats must be okay, too. Mommy says both are *pets*. And there it is. A new pattern, thanks to mommy. Pets.

Eventually, baby's understanding will grow beyond mommy's counsel to include goldfish, or parakeets, as well as names of favorite pets, and stories about them, and the sadness to be endured when a pet dies. What started as a non-human hairy thing that wasn't Uncle Morrie, became an assortment of animals, experiences and values. A theme of living creatures.

Patterns can be spectacular, at times. Not only do they help us identify the pieces of our lives, sometimes they provide a deeper explanation for those pieces. Which is crazy. The seasons of the year are a pretty basic example of this. Spring is followed by summer, then fall, and winter. But early in life, a child learns, the pattern of seasons may also be applied to measure other things.

For example, in spring plants are young and new, just like we are young and new. Summer corresponds to being an adult; fall is like growing older, and winter is like a season for death.

If we stopped there, we would have one pattern, and two possible uses for it. But it doesn't. You can also apply it to technology, or politics. The *pattern-of-seasons* can be used as a tool for prediction, and a powerful way to understand persons, places and things. It provides a million answers to a million questions.

Here's the point. It didn't have to be this way. Why should a pattern, like the four seasons, translate with such economy from one order to another? From a cycle of temperature-change, to the rise and fall of your life, or the Roman Empire, or the life of a star, or extinction markers for a species? The patterns-of-season ring out a hymn about time, from sub-atomic particles to dimensional membranes. And you can plug it in to just about anything.

Patterns inform us; patterns grow us; patterns connect us to the universe.

The *rule-of-pattern* is two-fold. First, it expects a degree of cosmic order; but of equal importance, it gives us a tool to explore that order. Two miracles that frame human existence, two miracles that didn't have to be, but are.

We succeed against the unknown for the simple, crazy reason: our old patterns plug into new things, and bring us revelation. This recursion seems to suggest, there's remarkable organization to the cosmos.

ThePattern

3 Narrative Patterns

Mommy and daddy told him *never go into the woods alone*, but when Pig Prince heard the voice calling, "Follow me, follow me," the naughty prince did what naughty princes do, he disobeyed and followed the voice deeper into the woods. But the wicked wolf jumped from behind a tree, grabbed the prince, and proceeded to escort him to a luncheon-appointment the naughty prince really would've preferred to miss.

The story ends with a daring rescue. The Pig King sends his boar guards to grab the prince, and the wolf runs away. Finally, a sadder-but-wiser Pig Prince returns home to his mom and dad, and the Big Pig castle.

At this point, I always asked the kids listening to the story, *what lesson did the prince learn?* Usually they would say, "Don't go into the woods." But the kid that won the literary prize for the day was the one who said, 'Don't disobey your parents.'" That was the moral of the story, or the *pattern-of-evaluation* I was looking for.

It has been the intention of storytelling, for who knows how long, to entertain, inform and-or prepare the listener for circumstances they might not have experienced yet; or provide a pattern for reality, of which they are unaware. There's always a beginning, middle and end to these things, but also, an important evaluation, the moral of the story. *Obey your parents. Eat your vegetables. Don't throw firecrackers at the neighbor-lady's cat.*

Closely linked to evaluation is a *law-of-understanding* known as *Occam's Razor*, the default setting for how many of us come to understand the universe. Occam's Razor suggests: the simplest, most succinct explanation is usually the best. In other words: *disobedience leads to trouble.*

Another example. Imagine an orchard. Most of us picture a line of trees, ordered across a grid. But when you see trees in a pattern, don't you also make an assumption? Someone did this. Someone conformed these trees to a plan. And do you actually have to see the person to know they exist? No. Because you just know: someone did this. Trees don't organize themselves in rows, on their own. The context suggests, there's an arborist out there somewhere, with a plan.

Occam's Razor slices through the more extravagant possibilities: swamp gas, the planet Venus, or a partridge in a pear tree, deferring, instead, to a simple evaluation succinctly based on what you already know to be true. *Someone laid out this orchard, intentionally.*

And this is pretty much how the universe gets explored. It starts in our instinct to compare the *unknown* to the *known*. A process that's automatic.

Stories, parables and analogies, then, give us a great way to contextualize our patterns. Patterns come with *values*. Values come with patterns. It's that simple. *Wisdom*, in other words.

Patterns repeated over and over, solar systems that look and behave to a degree like atoms, seasons of everything: recursive form betrays the unity of an arborist, a creative of spectacular range whose grand organization reveals His existence, whose patterns ultimately lead to himself. *God*, in other words.

ThePattern

4 Origins & Destinies

Since we're only human and not always as informed as we should be, it's nice that we can add *patterns* to those, we've already acquired. In fact, that's the goal of education. The more patterns you have, the broader your potential for understanding.

We can also revise our *pattern-evaluations* to match our ever-changing *Editorial Voice*. For example, your Editorial Voice may eventually challenge your evaluation of the wolf. Maybe wolfy would eat grandma, or little pigs like you when you're four, but when you're an adult, your Editorial Voice might re-evaluate the wolf as a noble, worthy survivor.

Of course, evaluations are tricky. For good or ill, the brain actively fills in any blind-spots in our patterns, based on editorial prediction.* And *we* are the authors and enforcers of those predictions. We tell our patterns what they mean, ultimately. We can tell them to lie to us, or take up with lazier standards and practices.

For some of us, editorial predictions link out to our parents; or more general themes like self-pity, conceit, intellectual pretense, or religious affection and the meaning of life. Whatever.

Some people say there is no meaning, of course: that everything's random and the patterns, accidental. *There is no intended order.*

Beware of anyone who advances a *theory-of-disorder* using an ordered argument. Be suspicious of anyone who dismisses *human evaluation* through use of *human evaluation*. This is intellectual treason.

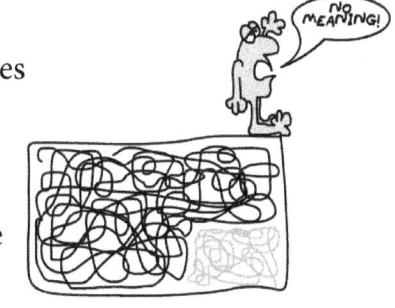

If there is no meaning to the universe, then the point you just made is ultimately … *meaningless.*

For many of us, the mere existence of repetitive patterns means something. And St. Paul said it perfectly in Romans 1:20: *For since the creation of the world His (God's) invisible attributes, His eternal power and divine nature, have been clearly seen, being understood through what has been made, so that they are without excuse.* (NASB)

Most efforts to sidestep the prospect of God fail to take into account the patterns that track Him across our consciousness, or the way the God-of-light shows up in the near-death experience. To believe in unintended order, we have to displace the values that elevated us safely from childhood. Patterns like, *I was put here for a purpose;* values like, *there is such a thing as 'right' and 'wrong.'*

The trails of God wind through our lives. We are based on His reference set, ultimately, which explains why we can never get past the *God-question.*

In the last coherent moments of our lives, we're probably not obsessing on the mass-extinction during the Cretaceous. Most of us are thinking about the local extinction of ... us. We're thinking about *origins* and *destinies* in the highest possible terms. We're thinking about God.

We see Him in the blessed, Holy patterns inside our hearts. He's there. His presence fills us with whispered proof of His existence. In moments of crisis, our native instinct is to utter a prayer to God, to call out for *help*. In moments of arrogance and self-confidence, we dismiss all communion with Him.

As it turns out, being human comes with the freedom to be stupid. Even so, even when we deny the Heavenly Father, even when we play the *wolf*, we're still beloved of God. After all, we are patterns of His making.

* Karl Friston, Predictive Coding

ThePattern

5 Patterns of the Soul

Starting with simple discoveries, we pattern our way forward, linked to the universe by humble comparisons. From simple patterns to great understanding, that's the magic. But something else happens. Inside our life is a *seed-of-presence* that is actually us, without our skins: our human *soul*.

Most of us have an intuition about the soul. For those of us who accept the idea, the soul is an invisible, second self. The question is, *what are we supposed to do with it?* What can we do with it?

Like seeds, patterns grow into the soul, shaping our beliefs. So, if this little *life-box* turns out to be the only piece of us that blasts off into eternity, we are responsible for building-out the soul with patterns and values that make it fly. A soul, rooted in light, rooted in godly patterning, launches straight and true.

When we were speaking earlier of the Editorial Voice, well, you could also think of it as the soul's *Master Voice*. When our patterns grow light, our Master Voice builds faith, the substance of things hoped for, the evidence of things, unseen. An invisible thing, faith, thus feeds the soul, also invisible.

Of course, if we cultivate patterns-of-darkness, they

change us too. Light becomes too simplistic for a darkened heart. As we drag ourselves off into blindness, our arguments in behalf of darkness bring us to hate the light. St. Paul talked about this (Romans 1:28-32).

Arguments in behalf of spiritual blindness:

> *erase well-lit expectation*
> *bring shadow to reality*
> *provide an alternative viewing angle*
> *invoke an optional perception*
> *sponsor plausible deniability*
> *invite eternal sleep*

The Master Voice is at the red hot center of who we are. It's never objective. It tends to rebellion. It lies to itself. But it's also free to make better choices.

To think about patterns is to think about the trail, outbound, and how the patterns we discover, build us. How finger-counting ends up as calculus. How the simplest discovery a baby makes, starts a pathway to bigger and better things.

But think about it another way. Think about the patterns inbound to our lives.

Why God created us is a great mystery, but even more mysterious, why does He love us and yet, consign us to a dimension where we have to interpret the patterns, where we have to engage our Master Voice in order to connect with His?

God uses patterns.

ThePattern

6 What Do You Say To A Fish?

Maybe … try a joke.

> Fisherman Hal asks a question:
> *What do you get when you cross a skunk with a*
>   *Myliobatiforme?*
>
> Fisherman Hal's punchline: *A stinkray.*
>
> Fish: *And what I really needed was a joke about a Halibut.*

Let's say, you've invented a technology that allows you to communicate directly with another species, brain-to-brain. All you need are a pair of magic gloves, a magic headset, and someone to talk to. And that should be the easy part.

So you head for the Grand Caymans and charter a dive to Stingray City, where there all sorts of possibilities. You pick out a big, prosperous looking stingray, lay hands on him, and start transmitting information. Assuming the neural-connection works, what kind of results should you expect?

Probably nothing, actually. For a tranfer-of-meaning to take place, you have to have – not just shared language patterns, you have to have shared *patterns-of-precedent.*

Try explaining, you've come out from the island by boat, you're staying in an expensive hotel on the beach, and flying back to New York, Thursday, on a 747. If you just launch into all this, without ramping up the patterns, your new friend is going to have a hard time keeping up. Without the latticework of patterns and precedence, you and the stingray live in completely different universes. It's something of a miracle that you can even see each other.

The stingray probably won't have much insight into the dimensions beyond his home.

There is an aerosphere above his kingdom, along with massive landforms, and a whole other kind of life. And it doesn't stop there. Go up 150-miles, and the aerosphere changes to something else. Go out a 1,000 light years and the universe starts to get really different from Stingray City.

But if you really want to drop a brick onto Mr. Stingray's head, explain the latest take on *String Theory.* Tell him, the universe is composed of atoms, subatomic particles, and ultimately, itsy-bitsy strings distinguished by frequency. And if that's not enough, explain that this line-of-thinking eventually brings us to the prospect of other dimensions.

Do you really think it's going to be easy to communicate all this to your new friend? Setting up a precedent-for-understanding is going to be a fantastically difficult mission.

But the stingray analogy is important because it goes a long way to describing our reality, as well. With Judeo-Christian tradition we are invited to see higher realities, *above the waterline*, so to speak. We are told of other realms and other forms of life, both good and evil; we are told of a Creator God who inhabits His own dimension, set apart from all else. In fact, the word *holy* means just that, set apart.

As difficult as it would be for a stingray to understand *String Theory*, think of the difficulty, communicating with the dimensionally bound, little blind tribe of humanity.

The higher intelligence would need to establish common-ground, the sort of thing that results from direct connection, comparisons, analogies, metaphors, and parables. And that's exactly what you find in Judeo-Christian tradition. And that connect-point, between the two realms, is a cross-point.

ThePattern

7 What Drives Cat Ownership?

We're coming up quickly on the boundary where the subject of patterns goes deeper into origins and destinies, and more speculation. Before we do that, though, let's do a quick review.

Somewhere in the deep space of every human being is a simple machine that performs nothing less than cosmic magic. It comes in two acts, actually. It compares stuff, then formulates a pattern based on that comparison.

It's usually already running when we're born. And while we may be able to optimize its performance through education, it runs in the background, investing us with a stunning harvest of information about the cosmos.

That's the main point so far. *We make patterns. We see patterns.* And when we stand back, we also notice something unexpected. Some patterns show up again, and again, and again.

Temporal objects, things that exist within time, tend to have springs, summers, falls, and winters about them. It seems to be a dimensional rule. But the point is, it didn't have to be this way. Once blackout is achieved, blackout should, or could be eternal, and it's not. That's curious.

After winter's death, comes spring, and resurrected life.

And the cosmic surprise is: at the heart of it all we find our simple machine pumping away. Starting with little, or nothing, it proceeds to grow our understanding of these things, and the universe. It is nothing short of stunning.

So, what about the patterns that come from this little *metaphor maker* of ours?

The first patterns usually contribute to a high-level, topographical overview for what will eventually define a complex system. A forest ecology, for example, might include trees, rivers, animals, and humans. The interaction of these components may lead to patterns of cause-and-effect, and maybe even the *who* of the problem, assuming there is one.

Another example. What about language? The ecological snapshot for language includes a brain, lungs, a tongue, and a number of unknown components and interactions. Though we don't understand everything there is to know on the subject of language, our topographical knowledge makes it, at least, explorable.

Let say, you come home, you find your husband staggering around, saying things like: "I want a cat. I've never had a cat. You … you have a cat, everyday."

topographical pattern

Knowing how much your husband hates this animal, you examine the *topography*, the *ecological view* for an explanation.

Now, if there are 30 empty beer cans behind the sofa, the ecology suggests a link between the consumption of alcohol and the neurotransmitters in you husband's brain.

In an instant you've got the: *who, what, when,* and *where* of this thing. And by the time you're finished with the boy, you'll have the *why*, as well.

If there are no empties, though, and there is a bump on his head, instead, the ecology suggests a slight concussion. And that's why he's talking crazy. That's why he wants a cat.

But if there is no bump, if there are no empties, the big pattern might be telling you, your husband had a stroke. The *ecology*, together with the sub-patterns of *cause-and-effect* suggest a link between crazy talk, inebriation, head trauma, and cat ownership.

In his book, *Modern Physics and Ancient Faith*, physicist Stephen Barr describes the discovery of a previously unknown particle, the Omega-Minus particle. It was predicted by *pattern*.

In particle physics there are two important properties known as *hypercharge* and *hyperspin*. In each particle, the mathematical characteristics defining these properties tend to be precise.

In 1962, researcher Murray Gell-Man noticed, when you graph these particles, according hypercharge and hyperspin value, what you get is a triangle; well, almost a triangle. Obviously, there must be something missing at the tip-end.

Logic tells you, there must be one more hydron, hiding somewhere.

And that's how Omega-Minus was predicted, and eventually discovered.

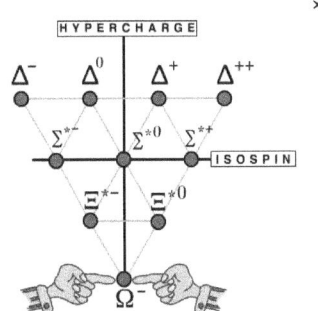

The pattern, an upside-down and slightly incomplete triangle, anticipated an advance in understanding. And that's what they do.

Patterns give us explanations. Patterns help us explore.

* *Omega-Minus graphic taken from* **Modern Physics and Ancient Faith** *by Stephen Barr, 2003, Notre Dame Press*

ThePattern

8 My Fulgurite My Faith

Sometimes, patterns help us with our understanding of big ideas. But where they can be really useful is *in terms of faith.* The result is not science, necessarily, but an important way to sort out our *God-questions.*

When lightning strikes a beach, sometimes it creates an artifact called a *fulgurite.* As the charge branches down into the sand, it leaves behind a glass map of the electrical pathway. The fulgurite – literally – flashes into existence with a big bang.

So, what if a lightning-strike is the pattern of analogy for creation, not the itemized, scientific explanation, not even a very good theological paraphrase. An *analogy?*
With all the necessary ingredients compressed into a cosmic *zap* file, God said, *Let there be light.* Instantly, the whole of creation unfolded, dimensions and time included, all sparked into existence like a fulgurite.

Time is the curious idea here. Sometimes we forget, time is a created thing, as well. And that's sort of the point of the analogy. When God said, *Let there be light,* He might as well have been saying: *Let there be time.*

Like a film projecting forward at a gazillion frames-per-second, time inflated to it's full measure as the stars and planets sketched into the timeline's path: birth-to-death, beginning-to-end.

Every plant, animal, every human being that would ever inhale God's breath-of-life would also explode into the timeline, start-to-finish; making choices; acting on freedom: all at the speed of lightning. And now, we slowly walk that reality forward in due season, chasing the time-tracks, lived and mapped at the instant-of- creation.

The *fulgurite* suggests one possibility with respect to how God could know the end from the beginning. But also, how we are free to make choices exactly as we define them.

No, the fulgurite is not a perfect analogy. It's theologically awkward, and a little illogical. But a fulgurite gives us a nice analogy for time and space, and a way to understand how God might actually exist apart from His creation.

An imperfect analogy becomes useful in understanding the biggest mystery of all. Jesus Christ, God Himself, entered the structure of His making, and lived as we live, then died as we die. His *communion-expedition* meant that He would enter time with us, then lead us out, to Himself, eternally. *Him to us. We to Him.*

ThePattern

9 Visible Light – Invisible Patterns

Light is complicated. It's also one of our most important patterns.

In terms of physics, it's a *two-in-one phenomenon* because it can be defined as both a particle, a *photon,* but it's also defined as a *wave.* It's sort of a difficult concept to understand. *How can it be both?* Well, ask your physics teacher.

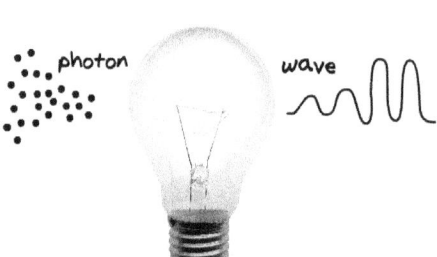

As it turns out, there is more light in the universe than we can actually see with the naked eye. Some animals see things we can't, up into the shorter wavelengths, into the *ultraviolet.* This world is close-by, dimensionally speaking, it's an overlay to ours, but it's a world we can't see, because our eyes start tuning out in about 390-nanometers. By comparison, snakes, politicians and some species of bats see longer wavelengths, into the infrared. Helps them with their biting, one suspects.

So this little notch of visible light is more than just a couple of hash marks. This is where we live. Our entire history is bracketed here within a boundary that marks human reality.

It would be interesting to know just how many patterns fill the world of visible light. If there is such a thing as *unseen* light, by analogy, could there not also be *unseen patterns* from other dimensions, patterns of the *cosmic* sort, just outside the range of our toolset? *The nature of God,* for instance. He has allowed Himself to be metaphored into things we understand on our side of the dimensional threshold, like a *father*, which suggests a lot about God's nature.

But if light is a *two-in-one,* according Christian theology, God is *a three-in-one*: a Heavenly Father, the begotten Son, Jesus Christ, and God the Holy Spirit, the Comforter. Like light, the three-part nature of God is a bit beyond our perception. Ask your neighborhood theologian about this.

And exactly where does the *three-in-one* God exist?

Way out past gamma rays and whatever else there is out there, the top-level domain is the zone of God's eternal presence where His glory is the ultimate illumination. And emanating from that zone are all the laws that govern the multiverse.

There are profound implications in this. The laws that prescribe light and gravity are interwoven with the laws-of-holiness, and in fact, are subsets of that holiness.

For Christian believers, this is the organizing principle behind the *Bible*, then, the *encyclopedia-of-patterns* from a higher dimension. By tradition, we separate two classes of law: one as an arbiter of science, the other as religious belief. But they're actually connected, parts of a unified creation.

From the moment of conception, we are outward bound, traveling up the ladder of the cosmos. And in the end, we break into God's eternal space whether we want to or not.

For Christian believers, the bridge across eternity starts with the cross on which Jesus died.
This is the deepest, sweetest pattern of all. A mystery. Given the many things our existence could be about, it is about the relationship of a Father to His children.

If we could look down on history from a *time-satellite*, we would see a trail of promise beginning in pre-history. This is the through-line of biblical record. A trail of Messianic light marks the path to a small child and a life that explodes in the glory of the Heavenly Father.

Christ was only active in public ministry for three years. Two-thousand years later, more than two-billion people, a third of the planet, consider themselves His followers.

When people attempt to understand how such an historically remote person as Jesus Christ lucked out in terms of influence, they tend to miss the important point. The blast from His resurrection *is still blowing across the planet.*

A teacher. A healer. A prophet. A brutal death. A cosmic return from the dead. A trans-epochal influence. Something big is going on here, in the pattern surrounding the Jesus-history.

ThePattern

10 X-Event-Worry or Trust

Every human has a snapshot of reality. Another way to think of it might be as the *island of you,* where the topography is made up of patterns; patterns of predictability, patterns of evidence and history, all the factors that shape how you think.

These patterns serve at the pleasure of your *Editorial Voice.* Think of it as the port authority that oversees which patterns get kicked off the island, and which are allowed on. Hopefully, your *Voice* quarantines you against wrong-headed decisions. Of course, if it's dysfunctional, it advances faulty understanding and bias, which are not good things.

In the ultimate sense, the topography of your life is created by you. If the ecology is sparse or unexamined, it's your fault. On the other hand, if it's rich and reasonably informed, you get the credit for that, as well.

Your Editorial Voice is absolutely you, and absolutely subject to the values you induct into your life.

What if there was an X-event that blew apart your reality? Your settled beliefs – once-upon-a-time – were shattered and disappeared, leaving behind a deeply wounded understanding?

What kind of X-event are we talking about here?

Maybe, a thermonuclear war breaks out, and hundreds of thousands of people are vaporized in under two-minutes.

Or maybe, the discovery of archeology on Mars, or the moon, and the announcement unbuckles everything in your reality.

Or maybe, millions of people disappear suddenly. Maybe it's a religious event.

Who knows what an X-event would look like, but more importantly, how would it influence the patterns that define you?

Would you go all catatonic on us? Lie down and twitch a few times and then die? Or would you take a time-out and restart with a revised snapshot-of-reality? Now here's the good news. Your Editorial Voice is fully capable of just such a restart.

One thing's for sure. There's more to reality than our patterns allow-for. The universe is massive, and the multiverse, hyper-massive and infinitely complex. And if we had all the patterns of the cosmos stuffed into our pretty little heads, it would probably be like setting off a brain-bomb.

God did us a favor by limiting our understanding, by not giving us all information about all things. In fact, the *Bible* openly states this: *Some mysteries are God's,* and for good reason.

The freedom that comes with having an Editorial Voice means that we have the sad freedom to blined understanding. And to blunt instinct.

For this reason, God set one last line-of-sight on Himself. *Recursive patterning* is the great missionary to our prodigal minds. Even when we look at a tree and say, "God didn't make that pine tree, it's just another gymnosperm, sprung from a long line of transitional forms to become what we see now."

And the voice of the Lord would reply, *And how did did this assumption arise? Did your reasoning happen in a random, disordered space? Or does your perception emerge from a naturally-acquired template that organizes. A perception that points to an arborist who sculpted all pathways through recursive order, with patterns that didn't have to be, but are. Patterns that lead to Himself.*

As you reassemble your snapshot, let your proofs be heart-proofs, based on the instinct and logic that calls to your soul, beyond words.

Lay aside your practiced rants against institutional religion and hypocrites. Their goofiness has no bearing on your communion with the Heavenly Father. Reassemble your patterns around a simple act-of-faith: *Taste and see that the Lord is good.*

If an X-Event happens to me, my plan is to go to the **Bible**, first. And which books of the *Bible* will I be taking most of my patterns from? *Matthew, Mark, Luke,* and *John*, probably. That's where you find the heart of God, pumping out in the open for all to see. And as for that X-Event, whatever it turns out to be, anything can be survived. And the *Editorial*

Voice is the secret.

Even when it seems, all is lost, your *Editorial Voice* can sort out the path that leads to the Arborist who created the garden.

For what can be known about God is plain to see, because He has revealed Himself to all. For His invisible attributes, namely His eternal power and divine nature, have been clearly perceived ever since the creation of the world in the things that have been made. So we are without excuse. Even though we suspectected, there was a God, we did not honor Him, nor give thans to Him, and instead, became funile in our thinking, and our foolish hearts were darkened.

Ephesians 1:19
paraphrased from the **Message Bible**

The End

Floyd Wray

Breakaway Literacy
1 The Roach of the World

We live in an age of breakaway literacy. Some might prefer to call it: the age of *broken literacy*. But both statements are true.

At this very minute, in a thousand coffee shops, people are pounding away, writing the next great novel. Drinking cappuccinos. Dreaming about their legacies. Living the life. But they are the ones who discover broken literacy, up close and personal. They'll pour their souls into a word-processor, then revise the narrative 30 times. It's hard work, executed over years and years, sometimes; and in the end, most of them won't find a publisher.

Then there's the alternate reality. At this very minute, a fourteen-year old is busy shooting a gross scene in a boy's bathroom somewhere, with a camera phone. And he will become the Samuel Johnson of a generation.

Why? Because he's smarter? The bottom line is: he's 14, and will merely outlive those of us sipping our cute little cappuccinos, wearing our cute little berets.

The fourteen year old is a little bit like the roach of the world, destined to survive anything.

Now if you're wondering, this is what *literacy* looks like. And here is what *breakaway literacy* looks like. Both are roughly equivalent.

Ultimately, *literacy* is about words and how they feed understanding. The problem is, we're not sure about how it all works.

It's strange that something as defining as language, as close to us as our name, can be so unknown. Our days are filled with words. We live by them. Die by them. But in the ultimate sense, we have no clear understanding of the intellectual mechanism, nor the editorial stress by which words are formed. Language just ... *is*.

Deciphering the subject, using words to explore words, is like exploring a cave with an echo. Language doesn't throw a lot of light on its depth or inner landscape. And to the roach, it doesn't matter, anyway. And that's why the roach survives.

Since we can't locate language inside a visible organ, or examine its atomic structure in a lab, we have to satisfy our inquiry with its *ecology*. We have to see it in terms of attributes. Not quantified by test, but defined according to practice.

One of the greatest mysteries involves how language began. We have text-records tracking how the written word emerged, but we lack any artifacts that explain how thoughts and words originally came together as spoken language. This merger is a big deal.

Some people believe, language had its origin in gestures and primitive barking. Others think, language began 350,000 generations ago in the mouth of a single language mutant, which quickly infected the surrounding population.

A number of researchers suspect that the headwaters for human language originates somewhere within the DNA sequence, perhaps *junk DNA*.

Finally, some of us believe, language is entangled with the mysteries of God. All four perspectives are legal.

Now, here's what we know.

Language is usually thought of in two ways. First, it's spoken in day-to-day conversation. The speech, gestures, facial expressions, inflection, all of it works together in a context to convey meaning to a listener.

The second form of language, the written word, records only the word-stream, not the context.

Language in *context*. Language in *text*. For most of human history it's been one or the other. Except, for more than a hundred-and-fifty years, a new system has emerged, one that records language in context; that is, spoken language, physical gesture, inflection, visual cues: all captured by *context records*.

These are the three cosmic events in human language.

Regardless of how the flow began, language is an unending stream of transformation. Whole civilizations have risen and fallen along its banks.

Greek, one of the drivers of enlightenment, relinquished its reign to Latin, which in-turn, transformed into the Romance languages. This is how language works. Ever moving. Ever changing.

But if transformation of spoken language is old news, there has never been anything even remotely comparable the *breakaway* fracture in language record systems over the last century.

Subsequently, we're stuck between two worlds. One filled with a legacy of pedagogic tradition; the other, in startup mode. One providing a window on the past; the other, a window on an unknown horizon. And sometimes, our time feels like the death of the human mind. Perhaps it's only being rewired. Which means, of course, *roach-hood for all.* Someday.

---

* *The origin of language is hotly debated. No one knows how, where, or when 'we' first came to practice speech. The notion of **350,000 generations** is an extravagent overstatemnt, though. Some theorists suggest that at the most, we came to language 200-300,000 years ago. No one has a clue.*

Breakaway Literacy

2 The Straight Line

When you're trying to convey your thoughts to some-one, a straight line is the best way in and out of the human brain, which may have a lot to do with why language tends to be linear: a simple point *A* to point *B*. Try telling a non-linear joke sometime, *A*-to-*U*-to-*H*, or something along those lines.

Is this significant? This linearity? *Well … yeah.* After words, it's one of the most important language innovations, ever. *Linearity* is a simple framework where ideas can be zip-lined into someone's head.

But there are other patterns, too. What comes out of your mouth is based on speech patterns you've heard from others. *Narrative input drives like-narrative output.* It's a rule.

Input-Output

Think about the way most conversations work. Someone will say something and you'll say something back. It's a natural response and often an *act-of-purchase.* Responding and repeating is a way of installing an idea into your understanding.

This pattern is at the heart of education. *Input* and *output* grow intellect.

What if you presented information to a child, but denied the child the right-of-interaction? *Input*, with no chance for *output*? *Presentation* without *cognition*?

Would there be consequences, intellectually? Sure. Denying half the pattern would interrupt the brain's integration of new ideas and probably damage the wiring.

Where Do Words Come From?

When you place an order for a cheeseburger and fries, and take a few extra seconds talking to the clerk, did you ever think about *where* the words come from?

Language connects to a number of points in your brain, we know that, including: Broca's Area, Wernicke's Area, as well as the Motor and Auditory Cortex, but your impulse to say what you say – *mustard and pickles but no onions* – what drives those sounds out of your mouth? Put it another way: where were those words hiding, two seconds before you spoke them? What ignited them?

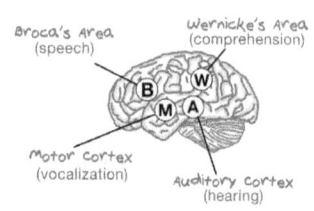

There are magical qualities about language, not the least of which is how we learn to build sentences in such a way as to be understood by someone else.

Descriptive grammar has to do with how people talk, the patterns of acceptable word order and things like emphasis and inflection, all the components that you see and hear in a conversation. Spend a few months in France. In addition to a rash, you'll probably learn to understand and speak conversational French, thanks to simple *input and output.*

Prescriptive grammar, on the other hand, has to do with formalized rules. Knowing how to speak French is one thing, but how to read it and write it, another. So read a thousand French books, and your output, your writing, will eventually reflect the *prescriptive rules of usage.* Again, *input-output.*

The first magic is that all these rules and classifications get adopted into usage through the input-output phenomenon that comes with our original equipment.

How does it all work? Where do the instincts for language originate? To be more specific, what drives our practice of input-output?

No one knows the absolute answer, but inside each of us, there seems to be a cave of sorts, from whose depths we contemplate, and from whose depths we also speak. Our shared patterns of language seem to be hidden in this cave with us.

Breakaway Literacy
3 Mouse Trauma

The point where the tongue and the soul connect is beyond exploration, for the moment, at least.

Everything we are as humans, both physically and emotionally, everything we are seems to be holed up in a deep space somewhere, where the anchor tenant is our DNA: the *Jacob's Ladder* across which humanity is draped.

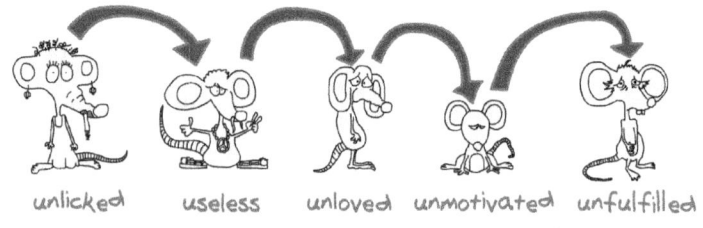

unlicked   useless   unloved   unmotivated   unfulfilled

A few curious, recent discoveries at McGill University suggest that memories of trauma can be passed from one mouse generation to the next through DNA-based memory.* And this might be important because of the implication. Could it be that we receive memories from our ancestors, then pass them to our offspring? It's not a new idea, it's just made a little more plausible through McGill University's *streaming mouse trauma*.

What makes it doubly curious, there's always been a suspicion that infants are pre-wired to speak the language of the community into which they are born. And the trauma-migration model suggests the pathway that would make it possible.

DNA may prove to be the ignition point for language.

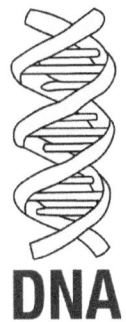

DNA

One other thing. There is a *probability calculation* known as *Zipf's Law*.** It's used by linguists and code-breakers when they discover a cypher made up of unknown symbols or glyphs. After running a Zipf calculation, the results predict the presence or absence of language, encoded within the cypher.

The point being: there is recursive, structural order found in all of the 6,500 languages on the planet. At some level, some deep level, they are related.

Using a Zipf calculation, a segment of DNA revealed that some kind of language seems to be hidden in, of all places, and perhaps even presiding over the DNA process itself.

In fact, not just one language, there may even be a second, an overlay of the first. This embedded form, this template, explains why certain patterns resonate across our use of language. In the final sense, language may turn out to be *DNA-reflective*.

Whether you hear it in conversation, or see it in the

written word, input and output are the pistons that drive enlightenment. In the mid-space, the client engages contemplation as they decode what's coming in, then code a response, an output, a purely cognitive process and a formidable transaction.

Input-output connects to our core. And fortunately, because of this, they are pathfinders as we seek to understand the technology-of-language, a language form, still under construction.

* Discover Magazine, Grandma's Experiences Leave a Mark On Your Genes, Dan Hurley, June 24, 2015

** Zipf's word frequency law in natural language

Breakaway Literacy

4 Authoring

Those mid-spaces in a conversation where we do the brain-work mark ground zero for enlightenment. With written records the same thing happens.

Of course, *reading* is a more demanding transaction than what you find in conversation. The intellectual rigor that drives it draws power from *assessment* and *evaluation*, characteristics that have advanced the course of civilization for thousands of years.

If the act of reading is the input part of the equation, the output side involves something known as *authoring*. Again, a rigorous transaction, certainly more demanding than what we find in a conversation.

Here's the interesting thing. *Speaking* often ignites understanding. We say something we didn't realize we knew, which is a nice feeling when it happens. But this is also the case when we *author*.

Maybe this sounds like the bleeding obvious, but the pattern of input and output – with respect to the written word – usually results in a higher level of accuracy. So, what exactly, makes authoring so accurate?

Well first, unlike conversation which usually tumbles out of our mouths with little or no contemplation, authoring happens outside of real time. A big plus when it comes to designing narrative. Authored words tend to be carefully selected. Specific. And when a written sentence doesn't line up with our intention, we try again.

A writer auditions a specific word or phrase, and if it works, so much the better. The editorial process allows *do-overs*. Iterations and do-overs endow authoring with power.

The reason for belaboring all this is to emphasize, human language is structured atop recursive patterns. Whether it's the spoken word or the written word, both classes share vital, structural points-in-common.

Based on this ecological view, we can model context records – an emerging system of narrative – as an overlay of the language pattern at its most basic and descriptive levels.

By studying the overlay, we see the deficiencies in our emerging technical grammar. At the very least, such comparisons can lead us to new approaches in education. And not just that. By understanding which innovations line up with our core, gene-level tendencies, we can more efficiently develop tomorrow's technology.

Breakaway Literacy

5 Context Records

Context records capture and play back descriptive grammar: voice, gesture, symbols, visual cuing, all of it transcribed as narrative in a *time-event*.

This is possible thanks to a second overlay of grammar, a grammar of *technology* and *specification*. This includes transistors, resistors, circuit boards, and of course, all the rules necessary to make such a system work.

It is a weird grammar in that it ignores spelling and punctuation – oh happy day – as it serves technical thresholds. And *no*, this is not the way we've done grammar in the past.

The system includes digital audio-video devices, film cameras, analog recorders, wire recorders, any technology that captures and plays back time-based narrative. These devices haven't shown up overnight. Context records have been around since before 1826, when Frenchman Nicephore Néipce took the first photograph from his bedroom window. In the years that followed, the system continued to evolve.

These devices weren't initially understood as pieces of an emerging language system. They just appeared from the mists as another interesting set of gadgets.

After 1910, as radio waves begin filling the sky with voices and music, the general public was awestruck, but few – if anyone – fully understood the implications. A new language form was appearing right before their eyes: first time in at least three or four thousand years.

For many of us, our first association with the emerging form occurred at the level of input. We looked at pictures, listened to phonographs, 8-track tapes, watched movies and television. The authoring was performed by someone else.

But remember that child, forced to accept input without the option of output? Well, while media observers offer a lot of explanations for the dramatic shift from traditional media platforms, today's brave new  world aggressively practices output, playing stingy when it comes to input-only media.

What we're seeing is a language system as it inflates the output side of *a new alphabet*, of sorts. Input is being shifted into balance by the rise of technically based output.

Breakaway Literacy
6 Crossing the Narrative Boundary

*Language seems to be embedded in our DNA, some-
how*
*We don't understand how it works, but from what we
can tell, it's based on a pattern of input and
output*
*Context records are a new addition to the language
system, and they line up, pretty much, with everything that's gone before; but they confront
us with a challenge: the challenge of translation*

In 1799, a French soldier by the name of Pierre-François Bouchard discovered the Rosetta Stone, a granite slab containing a decree by King Ptolemy V of Egypt, from 196 BCE. The text was written in three scripts: ancient Egyptian hieroglyph, Demotic script, and ancient Greek.

Since the content was roughly the same in all three languages, the Rosetta stone became the key to understanding ancient Egyptian hieroglyphics.

Don't understand a symbol, here? See if you can puzzle its meaning from the corresponding, parallel narrative, here. The Rosetta stone was the look-up table that broke the code.

It often passes without comment, but there is an underlying fabric, common to all human language, that makes translation possible. And it's important. The human family has generated an enormous library of narrative: our history, collectively, our science, our narratives of significance.

The trick for every generation has been to migrate information from the past into the present. More often than not, this turns out to be an act of preservation. Civilizations have traded knowledge, translating from one language to another since history began.

Unfortunately, context records don't necessarily follow the rules of translation. Unlike going from Greek to Latin, translating into context records involves jumping the very nature-of-grammar as we've known it, jumping into a new ecology where there are few theories-of-use.

Will the works of Tacitus – *The Annals or the Histories* – make the jump into context records? Or have they reached a final resting place as text? What about the writings of St. Augustine or William Faulkner? Or Cormac McCarthy?

Fortunately, there is a simple solution for translating into context, which is precisely what you get with an audio-book. And of course, there's also text-to-speech, an incredible solution to jumping the narrative boundary from symbols on a page to a voice-transcription.

Another solution involves *active listening*. Simply described, *you repeat the audio narrative as you're hearing it, shadowing the words with your voice*. Something you can do with any film or television program. And the exercise is an act of sensory cognition.

But the potential for context authoring doesn't end there. *Just audio* is *just the beginning.* And that brings us to a bit of self-referencing.

active-listening

Breakaway Literacy

7 Breakaway Literacy

The word *narrative* suggests a pathway. Maybe it's a conversation between two people, or a trail of words, graphics, or music.

Narratives tend to have *beginnings, middles* and *ends* about them; they also have bandwidth, comparable to lanes in a highway. The wider the highway, obviously, the greater the potential for traffic.

Do context records replace the written word?

Of course not. The written word is still *the heart that drives the beast.* Whether the words are spoken, or displayed as text, written narrative remains our legacy framework for whatever rhetorical form we eventually come up with.

Graphics and text, of course, have an age-old alliance, but the narrative in *Breakaway Literacy* was also rooted within a time-event, which had a huge bearing on how the title was constructed. And it was authored, which means it was revised, restated, and re-realized many times over during the course of development. And every revision rippled forward, bringing editorial change to all the different media-types.

By comparison, editing a text-based sentence involves a fairly straightforward transaction of *erase-and-rewrite*. When iterating a *context-based* sentence, though, the narrator must drive change across the associated pathways.

For some writers, this might come off like a deal-breaker, but it doesn't have to. To author super-narrative means that we'll have to become students again, if we are to add audio-visual sentencing to our palette-of-tools.

The visual side of *Breakaway Literacy* is not just animated sketch-work, either. The contextualized narrative is tightly drawn to the written word, added as a kind of *dependent* clause. We think of the end-result as a *scribe*.

When you are authoring a page of text, the game-plan boils down to forming a thesis, then supporting it with points-of-evidence. With a scribe, nothing changes. Since written words are conveyed through audio, though, it clears space for the thing that characterizes scribing the most. The author is free to create an additional *zone-of-intention*.

The whole idea is to broaden the bandwidth by amping up the language with diagrams, overstatement, understatement, and lame sight-gags, if absolutely necessary. Scribing frees an author to focus on tough subjects with incredible rhetorical firepower. It liberates dense content.

As it turns out, our eyes and ears are incredibly refined. The human receiver is powerfully tuned to sensory nuances. *Scribing* is thus perfectly suited to our on-board genius at deciphering things.

With so many media-types firing off on-screen, all the cues are driving a perceptual light storm in the brain.

With every new supporting flash of evidence, every explanatory word, the brain is hit with a massive thematic transaction. With luck, it will all lead to an increased understanding for the client.

Breakaway Literacy

8 Next Year's Words

The practice of language has crossed three milestones. The *first* marked its appearance. And frankly, there's still no consensus for how language began.

The *second* engaged the written word, and *written language* is still our prime tool-set for thinking and the transmission of ideas.

THREE MILESTONES

| 1
language
begins | *prime
toolset* 2
written
word | 3
context
records |

Context records mark only the *third* time in history, the human family have engaged a new form of narrative grammar. Rooted in technology, context records transact both language and time without the same formalized rules that govern the written word. But what happens when we take on a record system that changes the way we think? Our brains are still organizing the universe, the way brains tend to do, but the collecting and sorting of evidence has stumbled onto a new path.

Maybe the first thing to remember is: we've only just entered the *urban sprawl* of context records and are still between two worlds. The active window on the universe for many, employs screens and moving images with sound.

But our formal methods of education are rooted in a world that no longer exists as it once did. We are a world-culture in transition.

Authors will continue to build context-based exhibits with a deep reliance on text, for construction. And yet, through the simple application of *audio-to-text*, they can effectively translate from one narrative grammar to another through a highly accessible route.

To read the word and hear the word, as well, brings a doubled amplification to the user's brain. And *active listening*, where the client gives voice to what they're seeing and hearing, triples the amplification.

Another option involves *visualization*, the sort of thing you get with scribing. Visualization can be employed in two ways. First as *illustration*, where the image of a hammer, for example, represents a hammer, the tool itself. Many context records deal in simple illustration. The narrative components are pretty much unitized. *Hammers for hammers.* For the viewer, no deep perceptual deciphering is required, beyond allowing the narrative to *wash over* their senses, as opposed to *washing through*. But there's another possibility.

Narrative may also be a component in an analogy or metaphor, where the hammer represents … say … Germany, and the nail … Poland in 1939.

With a scribe, the visual and audio tracks often lie at a perceptual distance to each other. The audio tells part of the story while the visual tells another. And it's up to the viewer to complete the meaning.

There's usually a difference between watching a scribe and watching a film. Both are context records. They deal in *captured* or *authored* time; but one requires heightened deciphering, assessment, and *viewer completion*. It is in this distinction that visual analogy holds, maybe, the highest promise of all, because analogies can say a lot more in a lot less space.

A well-done scribe feels large, intellectually, and different, and slightly demanding. It has to be puzzled into place. And maybe the most interesting thing: scribes tap into an interpretive capacity, most of us didn't realize, we had.

In a word-cosmos with more than 1-trillion web pages, and an uncounted, valueless mass of words, scribes and multi-threaded media bring premium embellishment to otherwise word-naked narrative.

Short of an EMP-blast, the world won't be returning to what it was even 10 years ago. Both writers and publishers might be well-served to explore multi-threaded grammar, seeking new ways to tell stories and distinguish their *narratives-of-value* with context authoring.

Some of us will always prefer the smell of paper and ink, but much of the world is sitting in front of another window, now. And if we have a narrative contribution to make, we might do well to reposition our efforts to be seen through that window.

For last year's words belong to last year's language,
And next year's words await another voice.

T.S. Eliot, Four Quartets

LifePlanning
by Floyd Wray

LifePlanning
1 Scoping Out the Future

A few years ago I heard a sermon: *How to Know God's Will for Your Life.* The speaker was Dr. George Wood, and he'd done a lot of thinking about how to set up the plan for what you're going to be when you grow up.

There were two strange words in that sermon: *Moravian Pietists.** If you don't know what a Pietist is, neither did I. It could've been some kind of ecclesiastical tart for all I knew. But of course, an esteemed churchman like Dr. Wood, wouldn't be talking about ecclesiastical tarts. He told us, the 17th century Pietists were folks who sometimes, sought God's will by flipping open a Bible, pinning a finger to the page somewhere, then decoding God's will from a random scripture. Bible darts, except with fingers. But he reminded us, while the practice might not be totally defensible, well-respected believers like Lillian Trasher actually sought ministry confirmation this way. She went on to establish a legendary orphanage in Egypt.

He made another point. The little lady in the soup aisle, asking Jesus whether she should buy chicken soup, or beef, or vegetable: Dr. Wood said, as we piece together God's will for where we're going in life, soup is the least of our worries.

That Sunday morning I had a déjà vu moment. The sermon reminded me of a conversation I'd had more than three decades before. It took place back in 1969. One of my best friends and I were in a VW bus, Saturday night, A&W drive-in, watching girls, eating cheeseburgers–with 2000 fat grams – that was our tradition in those days. And from such a noble and lofty perch, an 18 and 19-year-old were conducting a discourse on the plan: *what we were going to be when we grew up.*

My friend was younger than I, but super smart and methodical. He told, me he was going to get his Bachelors (degree), go for his Masters, then get married. After that, he and his new wife would be youth pastors at a large church near a seminary, where he would get his Doctorate of Divinity. After that, he figured he'd be a missionary for 10-years. Then move back to the states and get a job as a professor, or a national director for a church organization.

He got more and more encouraged about the future as he talked up his LifePlan. My slightly less specific life map included making $1 million dollars, scoring a BMW, owning a nice house, and remembering to hold the onions on my next triple meat and cheese.

Some of what he was talking about hadn't occurred to me yet. The evening left me depressed. But it brings up an interesting question. How do you scope out the future?

Think about it. Every vocation gets rolled. Any plan you set up in here and now will have to take nourishment from a higher protein than you're going to find in the here and now. Which is not what my friend and I were doing. We were running on cheeseburgers–basically–exploring the future based on what 18 and 19-year-olds know about the cosmos. And in my case that didn't add up to a lot.

And let's be clear about something. This doesn't just have to do with being young. Middle-aged people hear about someone else's life-of-significance, and at night, stare out at personal disappointment, wondering: where's mine? Did I miss a turn? That 20-something kid with a BMW today, could Santa have accidentally missed my house and given my life to a rich kid?

No matter how perceptive or lucky we are, most of us eventually find out, any and all plans are subject to change. How many men planned to become riverboat pilots in the 1800s, only to have the railroad show up on them; or rail-roaders who got derailed when cars trucks and the federal highway system turned into reality? You can't control the future. And since the future interacts so unpredictably with all our plans, why even try? Why plan at all? How life and destiny interact is a huge mystery.

But consider reoccurring testimonials from the near-death experience. Where a person on the brink is confront-ed with a question, are you finished with your life's work?
Make what you will of the near-death experience, this seems to indicate that something big is going on inside your LifePlan. If these reports from the brink turn out to be a fact for the rest of us, *have you finished your work* may be

on everyone's exit interview.

For Christians it suggests, *God does care what we do.* Maybe our plan won't recast the space-time continuum, but it's not pure vanity that drives us to wonder about what we're going to be when we grow up. It's a God-created value.

We may not actually know for a fact what we're good for, or how our life serves the greater good, but most of us have a nagging instinct, we were put here for a purpose. Dr. Wood untangled the problem very neatly. And if there's an executive summary, this is it. God's will for your life begins in your character.

We would all like to see the big picture–where will I be 10 years from now, but it's generally the will of God, being lived out daily. *If I am in the will of God today, I can have the great confidence that I will be in His will tomorrow.*

* *The photo has been modified for purpose of illustration. Painted by Jan van Eyck, the original work was entitled: Giovanni Arnolfini and His Wife (1434). Any actual resemblence to actual Pietists is accidental, but intentional.*

LifePlanning
2 Is There A Higher Purpose?

Maybe we need to get something out of the way. Doing God's will is not about doing something you don't want to do, or turning into a twisted fanatic, pursuing a career only because it disgusts you. God's Word says, "Love the Lord with all your heart, mind, soul, and strength, and your neighbor as yourself." Dr. Wood said, *the word 'mind' was included here for a reason. It doesn't mean that in order to do God's will in our life, He takes a drill and neuters our mind, or scoops it out so it doesn't function.*

A life in communion with the Heavenly Father has a lot of latitude when it comes to decision-making. We get a sense of Heaven's perspective in Matthew 18:18, where Christ says, "What you bind on earth will be bound in heaven; and what you loose on earth shall be likewise loosed in heaven."

This suggests, the ongoing fabrication of *godly character* tends to lessen the risk of poor life-planning, and actually builds value in heavenly realms.

It's an interesting take on the subject for a lot of reasons. Mainly because it makes sense. God-enriched character wouldn't chase a cheap target. Right? And that goes a long way to explaining the verse in Romans 8:28: "All things work together for good to those who love the Lord and are called according to His purpose." Communion with the Father and the subsequent building of character give rise to *no-fault* LifePlanning. Why is this so profound? Because it suggests something we forget.

For most of us, the question is: *what will I be when I grow up?* You can be 50-years old and still asking that question. Except, it's the wrong question. What you should be asking is: *what am I today?* Because character reveals purpose. That's the first and most important thing to know about the big plan. Whatever it is you are to become, you are already becoming. Once you have this understanding in place, the next step is, whether to plan or not to plan.

Is having a map wrong? If you're not able to predict what's going to be happening five years from now, should you just toss yourself into the stream and see where it takes you? Well some of us do just that and it works, sometimes. Others, like my good friend, sketch out a course, assuming that good old human virtues like industry, thrift, and self-discipline will keep them on track. And sometimes that works.

LifePlanning
3 What Did Your Ancestors Know?

What if a physicist figured out a way to make a worm-hole. Not just your every day, run-of-the-mill wormhole, like you see in cheap science fiction.

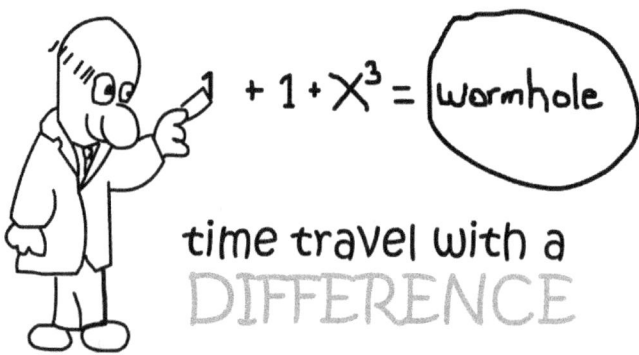

Time travel with a difference; time travel with video conferencing. Imagine dialing in all of your ancestors. Suspended in metaphysical space, surrounded by a 1000 generations of your people, what would you discover about yourself? One thing would probably stand out. You would be touched by the long string of humble, hard-working people who passed the spark of life to you.

There would be *repeater's*. Favorite uncles, seen the faces of men who lived two-three hundred years ago. And a string of mother's and grandmothers, big-hearted women who cooked, washed, managed, and bandaged, but could also swat a hinny, if need be.

And of course, there were criminals. Not to dwell on it, but some of your … *our relatives* were hung in the town square. Or shot at the wall, when the age of gunpowder rolled around. Here's the question: would your ancestors be as interested in you as you are in them? I could be wrong, but I think they would and would be willing to tell you about their lives: what they discovered from cradle to grave.

For some, a specific LifePlan attached itself at an early age. They hit the ground running. They seemed to know what they were supposed to do in life. Something that can be pretty upsetting for the rest of us, who don't. Across the generations, there's always been a tender spot between those who think they know what they're good for, and those who disagree.

A few of our ancestors may have had – strange is it may sound – *supernatural revelations* about the future. A dream or a vision of an explicit thing they were put on earth to do. Dr. Wood admitted, he'd always wanted to have a sign from God, like Paul on the road to Damascus. That is, until he noticed, out of the ordinary revelations usually came attached to trouble.

Prophetic windows were indicators that someone's life would be shaken to its core. When that happens, God's revelation from an earlier time would be needed as a ballast for faith.

Joseph had supernatural visions, and his brothers threw him into a hole, on account of: he was just more uppity than they could stand. All those dreams Joseph had as a young man, were eventually put to use when he was sold into slavery, then thrown into prison. Those revelations were eventually needed to sustain his wounded life. And of course, it was just that, the interpretation of dreams that brought him to pharaoh and a massive life plan that became *the nation-of-Israel-plan*.

If we had enough time to poll our ancestors, we would probably discover, most of them didn't have a clue what to do. Some struck a trail into fortune. Others walked into terminal illness or servitude. Their futures emerged in due course, seen a little more clearly in the tally at the end of every day.

Maybe they pursued natural inclinations, or interests, but they learned to be patient and watched for surprise. They would probably also tell you, there are blind curves coming at you. Some will be temporary. Some will wind on and on for the rest of your life. And you'll have to have a life-warriors flexibility to persist.

Our godly ancestors, who saw their futures emerge in the fullness-of-time, sought to understand their circumstance in terms of the Heavenly Father and the family-of-God.

When godly character is the basis for your plan, you have a resilience that is not your own. Sudden change has only a temporary impact.

LifePlanning

4 SANTAfication

When I was younger, I believed, if someone could just help me find square one, gravity or momentum would proceed to drag me towards destiny. And if gravity didn't do the trick, if my first move was right enough, I could ambush destiny when it crossed my path, assuming I recognized it. Which brings us to Santa Claus.

The *santafied* element in LifePlanning involves the passionat wishing that usually drives ambition. *Santafication* sets a material target, then *susses* out the appropriate steps to obtain it. Only one problem. The self-centeredness of the process, the unadulterated materialism it sets loose will probably not grow character. Anytime we binge on self-obsession, we expose ourselves to the very predictable risk of starving our souls.

Ask a rich person, if you don't believe it. Many, maybe all of them will tell you: wealth doesn't prevent loneliness, doesn't heal all disease, doesn't help with grief, alienation, depression, the sense of failure, or the worthlessness that can settle across your life. Sitting in your 50-meter Benetti in the middle of the Mediterranean, you can still be dying of cancer – totally lost to your value as a human being.

That's the 800-pound gorilla sitting atop the life-map for too many of us. Some of us are ultimately cursed because we succeeded with a treasure map concocted in an 18-year old mind, over cheeseburgers. Cursed because, purely human strategies enabled us to achieve purely human goals, but nothing else. No sense of completion. No deep happiness. The only thing we end up with is a nagging sense that we missed out on something.

What am I going to be when I grow up often turns into *is that all there is?*

LifePlanning
5 Lands You Do Not Know

Abraham, the father of Israel, proceeded without a life-map. God simply told him to go to a land he didn't know. Curiously, he wasn't given specific directions. God said, He would declare the destination. But here's something you don't hear a lot about. When Abraham finally arrived at God's will for his life, a homeland for his family, he walked past the destination, where God had led him, and into a wasteland, where the next thing he ran into was a famine. Then his relatives were kidnapped. Then there was war. All of it *after achieving the destination.*

For Abraham, *destination* and *retirement* were two absolutely different things. But doesn't that raise questions about God's provision? When you follow His leading, into a wilderness, then a famine? That's not what *religious voodoo* tells us to expect. But this is in the *Bible*, way up at the front of the book.

Abraham's great grandchildren, by comparison, had a map of sorts. Several hundred years later they were led back to the *Promised Land* by a pillar-of-fire and a cloud: God's GPS. Only this time, it took God's fire-cloud 40-years to get them back. But before we get distracted by the idea that God's little GPS strategy needed re-calibration, it was Israel that needed the re-programming.

God's mapping system was tuned to destination, but also: character, *national character*. Eventually, the artifacts of Egyptian bondage fell off – the scarabs, amulets, false religion, lack-of-confidence in the one who delivered them. What it seems to suggest, like Israel ...

we can have the map, but lack the character.

Character reveals purpose. Character reveals destination. Character requires purged motivation. This subject, knowing how to plan your life, is pretty much what Holy Scripture is all about. You find it centerstage in the lives of the prophets, priests, and kings, as well as the heroes and villains of the New Testament. But there is one super-set on the subject that transcends all other examples. And that is the LifePlan for our Lord and Savior Jesus Christ.

LifePlanning

6 How Jesus Approached LifePlanning

When I was 19, I never thought about Christ discovering his life. As that astonishing little baby rested in the manger, inside that baby, was there a presence looking out through super baby eyes, thinking: *cue the shepherds?*

How much did baby Jesus know? How much did He know as a kid growing up? As a teenager?

Scripture says, as early as 12, He was about his Father's business in the temple. That would seem to suggest, something was being revealed to Him by an early age. But here's where it's fascinating. As Jesus awakened to his mission, He never disengaged from the human family. Never once do you get the feeling that Mary would've called to Jesus saying, "What are you doing in there? Get out to the shop and help your father."

And you don't get the feeling that the Lord would have rationalized His behavior saying, "Hey I'm in here working on my plans for the triumphal entry. Tell dad I'll be out in a few minutes."

In those early years, character development was what was going on in His life. The Heavenly Father seemed to be revealing His will to the incarnate Son of God, as His character upscaled. How do we know? There's an interesting answer to this question, but first, a little context.

Fortunately, I haven't run into too many of these folks, but from time-to-time I've met a few distracted souls who loved people in other countries, but despised their own countrymen. For them, the *big plan* was over there somewhere, in the land of their empathy. Their brothers and sisters at home were not as important as their *big people adventure* somewhere else.

You never get the sense, the Lord was so obsessed with His larger mission, or timetable, that He took his eyes off the prize in the present. He didn't see His LifePlan or daily service as mutually exclusive. Of course, He knew, you were going to arrive on the planet eventually, and His mission was to redeem and bless you at a great distance. But you and His mission began in those who were weak and needy and living around him.

All great and godly life plans have this duality: *the big and distant, the small and near.* Our mission, whatever else it is, doesn't exclude our connection to the weak, lost, and dying around us. *What good are grand, cosmic schemes for destiny if they're based on the exile of local mercy?*

LifePlanning
7 Three Issues of Character

In Christ's run-up to the cross, three issues of character suggest that the will of God emerged from His study of the Word, and simple application of what He had learned. And curiously, or ominously, if you prefer, the testing authority on Christ's life plan was also the most evil force in the universe. Satan.

In the wilderness-temptation, the first issue presented by Satan had to do with hunger. After 40-days, not eating, the Devil encouraged the Lord to turn stones into bread. Had Christ failed here and done the deed, He would've been on course to betray the greater tests to come. Fortunately, Christ had done the homework. His reply came directly from the book of Deuteronomy: "Man does not live by bread alone."

The second question involved political *ambition*. Satan arranged for the Lord to see all the kingdoms of the earth. He said, *they're yours in all their splendor to serve your pleasure. I'm in charge of them all, and I can turn them over to whomever I wish. Worship me and they're yours. The whole works.*

Had Christ missed this question and chosen *a quick kingdom over in an eternal one*, He would've destroyed the promise of redemption: God's marvelous invention we know as *Grace*.

Somewhere in those invisible years, His character development had run a simulation on what happens to your head when you *aspire*. His character development had already purged His motivation with respect to fame and ambition. He answered again, from Deuteronomy: "Worship the Lord your God and only the Lord your God. Serve Him with absolute single-heartedness."

The third question was the big one because it targeted the most complicated issue the Lord faced. *Who was he?* Was He – indeed – the promised Messiah? It's a hard thing to understand because Christ was totally unique. There'd never been anyone like him. How Christ's nature was interwoven with deity was nothing short of a spiritual masterwork. But the human part of Him must've had some doubt at some point, or the enemy wouldn't have pursued this particular line-of-reasoning. He took Christ to the Temple heights and said, "If you are God's son, jump. It's written, isn't it, that He has placed you in the care of angels to protect you? They will catch you. You won't so much as stub your toe on a stone."

"Yes," said Jesus, "and it's also written: don't you dare tempt the Lord, your God."

Evidently the issue had already been raised and the conclusion sorted out. Had Christ failed the answer here, He would've betrayed the Heavenly Father. But more to the point: *betrayed the spiritual architecture of salvation that had been going on since the beginning of time.* Thanks to character development, the Lord wouldn't make the jump into presumption or demean the role to which had been appointed, with someone else's idea of how to test deity.

LifePlanning

8 Expectation

God's plan for the Son's life was constructed over 30 practically unknown years of character development. A blank space to us, but an astonishing period, evidently. From a mix of *scripture* and *communion*, Jesus Christ found the Father's plan for His future.

Are we worried about our plan because of the suffering it seems to invite? *Hebrews* 5:8 suggests that through his suffering, Christ learned obedience. He was the Son of God, but suffering was the fertilizer for His future, and at the heart and soul of our glorious redemption. There's another secret to the way Christ pursued his life. He had the great common sense to control His expectations. A lesser mortal would have been dazzled by the *what-ifs* in Christ's life. but He put everyone on notice, His expectation was, He'd be put to death.

Now, there's an uncommon ambition. We can run for decades in a service or sacrificial mode, but still have wrong-headed expectation of what's going to be delivered at the end of the term .

If our concession to serving God is governed by ambition and its demon-child *expectation*, someday we'll hit the wall. Take it to the bank. Maybe Saint Paul came to the same realization when he said, "I purpose to know nothing but Christ crucified."

Here's the bottom line. *Religious expectation often serves the court of ambition.* Unfortunately, it's often the executioner of true faith. You can run into disagreement on this point. A lot of good people argue, they're *ambitious for the Kingdom of God.* You know what they're trying to say, of course, but ambition, the *motivation to achieve* is not something for which God asks.

Even if your ambition involves building 100 Bible schools, or gathering every orphan of the world into your arms, no matter how laudable the ambition, it's no substitute for doing the will of the Father. It's not that orphanages or Bible schools are wrong, but there's an important nuance here, on which everything turns: God's will involves the preparation of your soul for its eternal journey, first and foremost. Then as you pursue the will of the Father, as you *seek ye first the kingdom of God and his righteousness,* these other things will be added onto you. Perhaps it's only semantics, but historical Christianity has – for 2000 years – crash landed on so-called *ambition for God.*

The only passion in which Christ indulged was to do the will of the Father. It wasn't an attempt at *achieving something noble* for the sake of achieving something noble, but the gutsy willingness to perform the expectation of the one who sent him, letting the Heavenly Father fulfill his *fathering* technique.

There is a difference between us achieving something, and being reconciled to do God's bidding. One of the greatest conversion efforts in history has been the attempt to sanctify ambition, calling it *God's will*. Which is a bit like dressing a pig in a tuxedo. In the long run, *expectation* that serves our desire to achieve, rather than a willingness to serve, however we may attempt to dress it up, usually leads to a long, dark night of the soul. Better to assume, there is no such thing as godly ambition. Only God's will.

LifePlanning
9 Devil Dog

My wife and I had a French Poodle when we first got married.

There were times, I was jealous of that dog. She had a soft bed. She had treats, whether she deserved them or not. And she was really easy on herself. She could afford to be. My wife and I had been put on earth to do her bidding. For all this easy benevolence, though, that dog had the rottenest core values of any dog we would ever own.

She was jealous, petty, sulky, vicious, high maintenance, and totally useless. But the life bestowed on her was precisely the easy life she came to demand. She was the potentate of a perfectly constructed little nest. By the end of her time on the planet, her expectations and demands – and our indulgence – had conspired to create a *devil dog*. Her life experience turned her into something gross. But it begs a simple wisdom. *Should we design a life that prevents God from practicing his fathering skills?*

Should we only aim to win personal ease and avoid risk? No one wants trouble, still Christ addressed the question. He tells us, we shouldn't worry about our lives: what we'll eat, or drink, or wear. Life is more than food, and our bodies are more than clothing. What's the bottom line, then? God doesn't care what we do, specifically, as long as we remain in communion with Him and allow Him to model our character?

Actually, it's more liberating than that.

Each person comes with gifts-of-interest and talent. Some of them might not be blindingly obvious, but they're there, like seeds: ready to give life to any number of vocations.

The point is: as you take personal inventory, as you look for a vocation that matches your special interests and skills, you have liberty. The God who knew you in the womb endowed you with many blessings, all of which are yours to use. Lawyer, musician, teacher, researcher – you are free to choose without fear because: *a life in communion with the Heavenly Father has great latitude in terms of choice.*

LifePlanning
10 X-Event

Learning not to worry, learning to trust the Heavenly Father is the ultimate answer to *what am I going to be when I grow up?* It is heart-and-soul, front-and-center, it is the core attribute in character development. And of course, a godly character is where your future begins.

Godly character is the province for all: butcher, baker, or candlestick maker. Assuming, we can view the future thru the eyes of character, can we at least afford to whine about what it's going to cost us? Or spend sleepless nights worrying about how well off everyone else seems to be?

It's probably a better idea to live fully in God-confidence; to cry out when things go completely off track and praise Him when they don't. But don't be surprised by the appearance of starvation and battle. Are you better than Abraham?

Bring faith to every surprise. Don't embarrass yourself with a plan that wins spiritual paralysis on account of your screaming need for security. Don't scheme around sacrifice, or rephrase ambition until it sounds like a feature. We have to use our brains as we pursue our lives. As we cast our nets toward the future, we shouldn't be delusional about our motivations

If you want to plan something, *plan to lose your life*. Lose it for the Lord and you will have used it most notably.

Friends this world is not your home so don't make yourself cozy in it. Don't indulge your ego at the expense of your soul. Live an exemplary life among the native so that your actions will refute their prejudices. Then they'll be won over to God's side, and be there to join in the celebration when He arrives.

1 Peter 2 (The Message)

Think of your suffering as a weaning from that old, sinful habit of always expecting to get your own way. Friends when life gets really difficult, don't jump to the conclusion that God isn't on the job. Instead, be glad that you are in the thick of what Christ experienced. This is a spiritual refining process, with glory just around the corner.

1 Peter 4 (The Message)

And if we ever come to a point where we don't believe what Peter is saying here, we've not only we lost a LifePlan, we've probably also lost a life, for no good reason. God's will for our life, our future begins in *character*.

Character requires purged motivation; character reveals purpose; and finally, character reveals the future, eternally. And if you're young, where should you start? As Henry Blackerby says in *Experiencing God*, "Look up, see where God is working now and join Him there."

Here's the big promise, the thing you can bet the future on, and the best hope for your LifePlan:

He who began a good work in you will be faithful to complete it.

Philippians 1:5-7 (NASB)

LifePlanning Notes – Journal
Preface

How important is employment? As a subject, it comes up fairly early in the book of Genesis (Genesis 3:19), where it's also linked to a curse. For some of us, this isn't a big surprise. For young adults – older adults too – employment presents us with one of the toughest questions we face.

00:20

While everyone wonders what they're going to be **when they grow up**, Christians often approach the subject from a slightly different perspective. They might say it like this: **What is God's will for my life?** It's interesting to think about how, adding God's will to the equation changes things. For some of us, it makes the proposition more difficult. Wondering what you're going to do is one thing; trying to ascertain what God wants you to do, quite another. Does God actually tell people to run chicken farms, or open a Mercedes dealership somewhere? Does He even want us involved in auto sales? If He does, does God prefer Ford products? The subject gets fairly silly, fairly quickly.

01:08

Throughout history, a boy usually followed in his father's occupational footsteps. The options might have included farming, or a craft like carpentry. **A person's working-life thus began in the lives of their parents. Boys did what the men had always done. Girls did what the women had done. Across history, our ancestors were usually locked into an occupation with little choice in the matter.** Of course, vocational migration was always possible through education or membership in a guild, but it was the Industrial Revolution where our work-traditions changed drastically. People moved into the cities. A farm-boy could study medicine. A carpenter's daughter could become an astronaut. Here's why a distinction between past and present is important. **Historically, God-fearing believers haven't had the luxury of**

getting too confused about what God wanted them to do in life. In order to survive, **they had to do something, or starve.**

Where do we start? What are the guidelines we should follow when chasing down a vocation?

02:18
Occupation, Avocation, and Collision
Sometimes, occupation and avocation collide, resulting in outcomes that are completely unexpected. One of the best examples is found in the New Testament, where Christ enlists his first four disciples: Peter, James, John, and Andrew. Fishermen. When Christ walked up that morning, they were already on-the-job, with a full day's work ahead of them. Christ interrupted their vocation with a simple invitation. *Come, follow me, I'll make you fishers of men.* (Matthew 4:19, NIV) That's all it took. For these four Galilean fishermen, their vocation changed to an avocation in an instant. They walked away from their nets and **walked into history's most stunning event.**

It's legal to ask what Jesus saw in these guys. You don't get the sense they had much insight, beyond their vocation. On the other hand, what they knew about fishing seemed to be a recommendation. There was an art to fishing, not unlike the art of capturing lives for redemption. Even more significant, Christ chose fishermen over the teachers and preachers that filled the streets of Jerusalem. **Why didn't Christ start His mission using religious people?** The answer to this question should bear a corrective message for our communities of faith, today.

03:44
These four men from northern Galilee were **unlearned and unknown to the professional classes in Jerusalem.** They spoke with country-accents. Still, they were precisely the people Jesus

needed for His mission. Their quick response is especially compelling when you compare it to the passage in Luke 18:18-23, where Christ extends a similar invitation to a man known as the rich young ruler. By contrast, Peter, James, John, and Andrew were able to step into line behind the Messiah, and **abandon life as they had known it.**

04:26
Vocational Realities
There's absolutely nothing wrong with bringing our lives to the Lord in prayer, seeking His will, His direction, and blessings on what we do. This is a grand tradition among God's people, and quite frankly, one of our greatest privileges. As simple as it sounds, though, some of us are tempted to add liturgies and methodologies to what should be a **humble presentation of self to the Heavenly Father.** The Moravian Pietists were probably well-intentioned in their efforts to integrate Holy Scripture into their decision-making, but flipping pages and pointing randomly at the page was not the highest, best use of scripture. Think about how much guidance is available in the Bible. Abandoning God's intentional narrative for what amounts to a game of Bible-darts-with-fingers is a complete waste of God-breathed inspiration. **There are answers in scripture. Chase them down;** don't chase the end of an arbitrary finger.

05:35
But there's something even worse than Bible-darts and bogus methodology. Christianity has always been in a tussle with itself over how to make God relevant to the modern mind. Again, such intention might be understandable, but **God doesn't need our efforts** in public relations. He represents Himself quite nicely, thank you very much.

06:01

Specifically, vocational destiny is often presented as one of the reasons to give your heart to God. We ought to pause on that one and think about it for a second. Will being a Christian bring you a better job? It might, but it might not. When we step in line behind the Lord, there is a change in the way we conduct business. Improvements are definitely going to show up. The big thing about being reconciled through Christ, though, is that **we cease trying to be God**, and **humble ourselves to the marvelous task of seeking Him.** We follow His commands. We live as He taught us to live. **Communion with the Heavenly Father through prayer and the study of scripture, changes us gloriously** and completely, all the way to the sub-atomic level, maybe. Who knows? And if our vocational reality improves, to God be the glory.

06:59

On the other hand, the promise of a gold-plated lifestyle is a completely bogus inducement. Our **vocational ascendency is not why Christ came to die.** Some public speakers are completely out of their minds on this point. Out of their minds. If you refer to scriptural record, certain things pop out at you.

For one thing, followers of Christ **don't necessarily have it easier** than everyone else. Christ was crucified. Should those who follow Him be surprised at the cross they're privileged to bear? **Christ had no place to lay His head.** Should those who follow Him expect a five-bedroom home on the 18th hole, with a four-car garage and a private landing strip? And French poodles?

07:48

Through His suffering, Christ learned obedience. Should we expect to join His mission and be exempted from His suffering? St. Paul says: … we share in his sufferings in order to share in

His glory. That verse is found in Romans 8:17. This isn't welcome news. And bringing it up at this point isn't intended to cast a wet blanket over the joy of new life in Christ. There is an amazing difference that comes into our reality when we step in line behind the Messiah. But **Christ's mission was about eternal life, not indulged life.** How does this impact our approach to LifePlanning?

A Personal Quest
Some of us endeavor to apply our most **logical analysis** to the *what am I going to be* question. Way back in the mists of late childhood, my highest thinking on the subject revolved around: **which occupation promised me the most money; which job came with the most long-term security?** You would be right in arguing that these were not the most enlightened questions, but most of us start the process with this perspective, if we're honest about it.

09:03
My second level of analysis involved whether or not I had what it took to do a particular job. Many of my favorite vocational prospects were assassinated by the words: *if you're good at mathematics and science.* Like most of my friends, **I liked the lifestyles that came attached to all sorts of job descriptions, but not the work to which they were attached.** I had good reason to suspect my limitations. Little wonder that by my late-teens, I had pretty much given up on all prospects for a dream job. Most dream jobs required a level of brainpower, I was fairly certain, I lacked. I eventually came to the conclusion that **whatever I did, vocationally, would have to happen by accident,** or some other means not known to me. I had a pretty low estimation of my perceptual-resources. That, and I was seriously lazy.

1
SCOPING OUT THE FUTURE

LifePlanning Notes – Journal

It was God's great blessing that I had a friend who was my exact opposite in this respect. Before he was a senior in high school, he'd laid out a LifePlan of staggering breadth. He hadn't sketched it out on a spreadsheet, but he was **incredibly organized on how he planned to conquer the next ten years.** Ultimately, he succeeded; he achieved the goals he'd set for himself back when he was in high school. This still stuns me.

00:31
The thing about vocation, **sometimes our plans work, but sometimes they don't. Sometimes no plan at all is the best plan of all. Sometimes, it's not.**

We've been challenged teachers, preachers and counselors to discover **our strengths.** There's probably nothing wrong with such an inventory, but when we finally have our list, what's it good for? Have we really advanced the mystery of LifePlanning to any great degree? According to Biblical history, the first four disciples weren't chosen for their wealth of self-knowledge. Peter was a fairly goofy character, all things considered, but Christ saw something in him, Peter could not have seen in Himself: a man who could drop his nets and follow, in an instant; a man whose simple faith made it possible for him to jump out of the boat and attempt to walk on water. These were Peter's strengths, and there's no way to self-test for such things.

01:34
St. Paul said it like this: "Therefore I am well content with weaknesses, with insults, with distresses, with persecutions, with difficulties, for Christ's sake; for when I am weak, then I am strong."
(2 Corinthians 12:10, NASB)

Seeing The Future
Implicitly, there's a huge problem with scoping out the future.

No one can accurately foresee what happens next. In the mid-1800s, guys like Mark Twain wanted to be riverboat pilots. At the time, the assumption was, there would always be a need to convey people and goods from one place to another, which was true enough. What guys like Twain might not have seen coming was the railroad. By the late 1800s, the prospect of being a riverboat pilot had lost a lot of its appeal. Instead, people wanted to work on the railroad. Had Samuel Clemens – Clemens had given himself the pen-name of *Mark Twain* – had Clemens been born 30-years later, he might have named himself … *Mark Train*. Of course, trains are still part of the transportation grid, but what you couldn't have predicted in the late 1800s was the upcoming prominence of cars, trucks, and the appearance of the federal highway system.

Is there a pattern? Of course there is. When choosing a future for yourself, remember: through no fault of your own, **your most enlightened choice could still put you on dead-end street**, vocationally. Or render your clever nom-de-plume, an antique.

03:26
Mistakes of Youth
By our late teens, many of us believe that we're expected to know what we're going to do for the rest of our lives. **Not knowing and admitting it** can be stigmatizing. It can also be dangerous. **Anxiety over the future can be a great motivator, but it can also stampede us into a wrong-headed decision.**

03:51
There's another possibility. Sometimes, the career path we choose in our twenties turns out to be the most hateful thing we could've ever done to ourselves. **Young-brains can indenture us to employment-prison.** Many 40-year olds come to this conclusion. But how do you plan for a future when no one knows what

LifePlanning Notes – Journal

the future looks like?

Maybe it sounds funny, or even tragic, but many of us in our 50s, 60s, even 70s, **carry around a phantom** from youth. Though we're way past the starting line, many of us are still searching for *what we're supposed to be when we grow up.* Either that or, we wonder how things might've been different had we taken a different path?

By the way, have you noticed the overall tone here? LifePlanning is starting to come off as a tad hopeless. Which is precisely the point. The difficulties confronting us, with respect to what we're going to be, may actually be whispering another message, a message we might not expect.

What if God's will for our lives is something entirely different from what we think it is?

05:08
Reset
According to Paul, God's will is simply this, that: *all men be saved and come to the knowledge of truth.* (1Timothy 2:3-4, NIV)

After Christ, Paul's was the most powerful voice in Christianity. He sojourned from one end of the world to the other, fearlessly proclaiming, Messiah had *come to redeem us.* And lest we forget: **occupationally-speaking, Paul made tents.** He had been educated under the great rabbi, Gamaliel, but his day-job involved the creation of nomadic housing.

05:49
Of course Peter, a professional fisherman, said roughly the same thing about God's will: "The Lord is not slow about His promise, as some count slowness, but is patient toward you, not wishing

for any to perish but for all to come to repentance." (2 Peter 3:9, NASB) Neither man dedicated much ink to their strengths, occupationally-speaking. They did what they did: fished or mended tents, but their alpha-mission in life – their avocation – was something else entirely. They were Christ-followers who also worked. For Paul, God's will was that he *wouldn't perish, eternally.*

06:36

Does God want you to be a doctor, or a lawyer? Or a teacher ... or ... whatever? The jobs we undertake are important to both God and us. That said, though, scripture seems to suggest that God might have an even more vital expectation for you. The evidence fills every page in the Bible. At its most basic, God's will is that none should perish; and the functional, Biblical prescription for not perishing involves **God's supreme interest in your character: the sum of your spiritual, ethical, and moral qualities.**

07:19

Character First

The shock-announcement that **character comes first might seem a little unexpected.** On the other hand, a pretty compelling argument could be made that the whole of scripture promotes the subject. Isn't character the theme that pops out of the Biblical account featuring Adam and Eve? Disobedience? Noah ... obedience? Jonah ... both?

Christ was once asked to reveal **the greatest commandment.** You find His answer in Mark 12:28-34, and in Matthew 22: 34-40. His answer was simple. He said that *we should love the Lord our God with all our heart, mind, soul and strength, and our neighbor as ourselves.* This commandment radically impacts character. If the dictionary definition of character is based on

LifePlanning Notes – Journal

the attribution of *ethics and morals,* Christ's words expand the definition to include the *love-of-God.* There's a big implication in this.

08:33

Perhaps we should clarify something. Personality traits are usually thought of as the tendencies or natural attributes that define you. **Character, by contrast, describes your efforts at reforming those traits.** If you've an inclination to selfishness, the fix involves an intentional effort. Pursuit of godly-character resets your tendencies. Ultimately, the laws God prescribed to Moses are anchored in character. And there's a caveat. **YOU are in charge of applying godly principle to your behavior.** Character is in your portfolio. It's yours to moderate. Ultimately, no matter how devoted we are to the godly-recasting of character, God understands, our efforts require a divine-assist. It gets a tad theological, but it boils down to a fairly simple list.

09:32

> *God's will for your life begins in your love for Him*
> *If you love Him, you'll keep His commandments*
> *His commandments were created to help you with the*
>   *advance of character*
> *His Son's redemption, and the grace it brings, fixes the*
>   *part of your character that lies beyond your reach*

When a person's character lines up with God's standards, everything finds its place. Where will we be 10-years from now is not as important as where we are, today. In that respect, the godly-honing of character assures that *if we're in the will of God today, we'll mostly likely be in His will tomorrow.*

2
IS THERE A HIGHER PURPOSE?

LifePlanning Notes – Journal

Good fortune. Bad fortune. Health. Sickness. All things work together for the good when we're in vital communion with the Heavenly Father. **At the end of every trial or affirmation, we walk away, improved.** Admittedly, this challenges the more popular brands of voodoo-spirituality; voodoo that says: *God wants us rich; God wants us to have our ease; God grants exemptions from suffering.* Now, exactly where is this voodoo-doctrine found in the Bible? Hebrews 11:36-38, perhaps?

00:48
"… and others experienced mocking and scourging, yes, also chains and imprisonment. They were stoned, they were sawn in two, they were tempted, they were put to death with the sword; they went about in sheepskins, in goatskins, being destitute, afflicted, ill-treated (men of whom the world was not worthy), wandering in deserts and mountains and caves and holes in the ground." (NASB)

The Bible **is bad news for those of us who seek pampered indulgence.**

Curiously, when circumstance forces us to deal with grim reality – on the way out to the garden to eat worms – some of us adopt a reversed mental picture of God's will as something unwanted, awkward, or invasive.

Does God actually want us in pain? Does He want us, poor? Does God want us dismissed, or diminished? Does He like it when we lose?

Such notions miss the point by a cosmic mile. If God's will targets an upscaled character, why would He seek our annihilation? It is true, character-building often results from tough circumstance, **but that doesn't mean God wants us to conduct** our lives *oriented to trouble.* He wants us oriented to Heaven. In Philippians 4:11-13, Paul explains it quite clearly.

"I've learned by now to be quite content whatever my circumstance. I'm just as happy with little as with much, with much as with little. I've found the recipe for being happy whether full or hungry, hands full or empty. Whatever I have, wherever I am, I can make it through anything in the One who makes me who I am." (MSG)

Taking Paul at face value, **what God seems to expect from us is a simple, clean, totally natural approach to life, based on confidence in Him.**

02:44
Cars In The Barn
A few years ago there was a wonderful myth floating around the Internet. Car-geeks, myself included, were captivated by the tale. According to the narrative, a guy bought a small tract of land containing a house and a barn; and he was chiefly interested in the land, so he didn't take time to go into the barn until after the purchase. According to the tale, he used a cutting torch to open the door. Once inside, he found the barn filled with rare automobiles. The scope of the treasure became known only after someone with a camera and a flash unit roamed the aisles shooting pictures of the vehicles.

03:26
Those flashes of light brought definition to a scene, otherwise lost in darkness. Treasures in the shadows were revealed with each burst of light. **So it is with the flash-points of character.** Every time life presents us with an unexpected challenge, we get to see those bits and pieces of who we are, otherwise hidden

LifePlanning Notes – Journal

from view. Some of our characteristics are full-blown treasures. Some aren't. **Flash-points alert us to issues that need to be addressed, spiritually. They can also reveal the future.**

04:04
Reveal the future? How does that work?

As we allow the combination of God's word and the Holy Spirit to recast our weaknesses, **cheap targets are disclosed for what they are.** Yesterday's selfish fantasies start to look ridiculous. Maybe even corny. **As character upscales, we have the chance to clear the deck of our conceits.** We have clarity. Our spiritual eyes start to focus on the future in terms of what God wants us to be when we grow up.

04:39
As It Is In Heaven
This brings up a subject that's a little fuzzy for many of us.

Is God's will done on earth? After all, if God is in charge of the cosmos, when something happens, it happens because that's what He wants. Right?

Not necessarily. By that logic, the slaughter of six-million Jews during World War II would be something God wanted. And if that's not bad enough, the murder of children, terminal disease, and all the devastating realities that show up on a regular basis, become the handiwork of God.

05:21
When you read the book of Genesis, you discover, there's another force in the universe. A *thing*, actually. It has a distinct personality and is at war with the Heavenly Father. Satan's goal **is to**

subvert God's plan by any means possible, and the medium for his dark-artistry involves God's little blind-tribe of humanity. His behavior toward us is despicable. He does His best to interrupt our association with the Heavenly Father. And guess what? His principle tactic is to short-out the wiring that connects us to God's will.

06:01
But if God is the all-powerful overlord, why does He allow Satan to continue his dark practices? **If God can do something about evil and doesn't, God becomes the source of evil.** It's a topic that stumps the best minds. Not only do we lack the answer, we probably won't even understand the question completely, until we reach the eternal domain of the Heavenly Father. **It's an issue that will taunt us, but also grow us, until then.**

06:33
There's evidence of an answer, though, in scripture. The most revealing hint is found in the Lord's prayer, which is found in Matthew 6:9-13, and Luke 11:2-4.

"Our Father who art in Heaven, hallowed be thy name; thy kingdom come, thy will be done, on earth, as it is in Heaven ..." (KJV)

Most scholars see Christ's words as suggesting, God's will is not necessarily done on earth. But how would that work?

When we unpack the problem, we realize, **there are all sorts of wills being practiced on the planet.** As a matter of fact, **freedom-of-choice may end up being God's most nervy creation of all.** It means, we can **choose to love Him without coercion,** and that's quite a beautiful thing. It also means we can choose not to love Him. And that's where the trouble begins.

LifePlanning Notes – Journal

If it is true, though, if His will is not necessarily performed on earth, why do we seek God's intention?

07:42
To help our understanding here, let's set up an imaginary situation. **Your husband has been laid off his job.** Your savings are depleted and there's no one to whom you can turn. Out of nowhere, your husband's old supervisor calls and tells him about **a new job-posting.** The job starts immediately, and it's right in line with your husband's vocational track. Given the fact, this opportunity came out of the clear-blue, it would definitely seem to be God's solution for your problem. **And it may be. But the job still might not happen. There's God's will. There's our will. And then, there are the wills of third parties.**

What if the big boss at your husband's old company wants a dream-job for his new son-in-law? What if you wake up Monday morning to the crummy reality that someone else got the job? Viewed from a certain angle, it might seem that God's will isn't as potent as it should be. **But if God doesn't force you into a relationship with Himself, is He going to force your husband's ex-boss into a decision that revokes his freedom-of-choice?**

08:53
The only thing we have any control over is our will, and how it lines up with what God wants. This is the precise dynamic behind Paul's statement that he had learned how to live with wins or losses. *In either case, I can make it through anything in the One who makes me who I am.* Philippians 4:13 MSG)

09:14
God's Plan
Over the years, I've had difficulty, keeping a fix on the specifications surrounding God's will. **If I see an option, and it's attrac-**

tive, I induct it into my expectation as God's next, big thing for me. I lose the bit about His interest in my character, and almost instinctively detune my understanding to the level of *things* or *events.* In an attempt to improve my resolve, I've sought biblical context for this question. I'm no theologian, so what follows is more of a personal observation, not a grand, theological argument.

09:56

Our role in the cosmos had an honorable beginning. God created a life-form specifically designed for communion. The plan was to have a human family that pursued Him in terms of love, without being forced to love Him, by edict. **God wanted us to seek Him out with the natural affection and curiosity, a child has for its parent.** When Adam and Eve betrayed communion, through disobedience, they were punished, as children are punished. What we take from this: **God's will was breached by human choice.** Even so, His plan didn't change, overall. He still wanted communion with His blind, little tribe.

Satan played a huge role in this mess-up. According to the first book of the Bible, he tempted Adam and Eve to disobedience. It resulted in God's judgment against all three. (Genesis 3:14-17)

10:53

As I searched for other biblical examples, I found the pattern repeated over and over. It's seen again in God's plan for a chosen people. God made covenant with Abraham, and subsequently, Israel. *If they followed in His ways, He would protect, bless them, and make of them a great nation.* Ultimately, **from Israel's bloodline, God would bring forth Messiah, a second Adam,** to reset the calamity created by the first. This is found in Genesis 3:15. But Israel botched their end of the covenant with stunning con-

LifePlanning Notes – Journal

sistency. **Their acts of free will inevitably frustrated the grace of God.** Even so, His commitment was never revoked. More importantly, His plan to send the Messiah, never retracted.

No stretch of the imagination is required to understand the triangulation here.

11:56
God's will. Our will. The will of third-parties.

What I never expected from biblical record, though, were the unintended consequences, or as I like to think of them, the *tumble-up phenomena* that often accompanies a breach in godly design. The most notable example is found in the life of Messiah.

12:17
As always, the evil-one attached himself to the enterprise of salvation. He targeted the religious/political leaders in Jerusalem. He also went after Christ. As usual, his tactic was to get everyone off-course and trash God's intention. In the end, **he achieved an unintended consequence** for himself.

12:39
In a way, he won a small victory. He influenced human will in the crucifixion of Messiah. But the result was a **tumble-up transaction**, with respect to outcome. If God's plan had been truly fragile, the murder of Christ would've put an end to the mission, but **God's plan** – perhaps unknown to the evil one – **contained a blueprint for** resurrection. For the enemy, the conspiracy against the Heavenly Father blew up in his face. He ended up, conspiring against himself in what has to go down in history as the *grandest of all unintended consequences.*

13:19
When we find ourselves trying to figure out what's going on in our circumstance, there's a temptation to see God's will for our lives as **fragile and perishable.** Actually, if His will involves character, **everything the enemy throws at us has the potential for improving us** – blowing up in the Enemy's face, instead. Even if the boss' son-in-law gets the job, your husband won't be abandoned by God. It may feel like you've come to the screaming-end, but God stands by your side.

13:53
In retrospect, we often see **a whole string of blessings that proceed from what began as a perceived breach in God's will.** This is stunning. It says a lot about why Paul admonishes us to **persist in tough times,** to keep running the race. Opting out of our commitment when prospects seem to detonate, jeopardizes the resurrection part of the equation: **the unintended consequence, the *tumble-up* phenomenon.**

"Keep your lives free from the love of money and be content with what you have, because God has said, 'Never will I leave you; never will I forsake you.' " (Hebrews 13:5, NIV)

14:37
Nazi Germany
I can't leave the subject of unintended consequence without a quick visit to my favorite, non-biblical example.

Over the millennia, **Satan has continued to inspire bloodshed and betrayal.** A prime example is the Jewish Holocaust in World War II. This terrible event has haunted me since childhood, sometimes ambushing my allegiance to the Heavenly Father. *Why did He allow these marvelous people, His people, to suffer at*

LifePlanning Notes – Journal

the hands of the Nazis?

Part of the answer lies in understanding that **such things are the direct expression of human will, not God's. The freedom by which we bless may also be the freedom by which we curse.**

15:24
As I was studying the history of World War II, the pattern emerged again.

Here's the background. After the first World War, Germany was severely punished by the Allies in the Treaty of Versailles. The Germans lost land, wealth and self-determination. In those years of hardship, the German people came to feel, they'd been sold out by their leaders, and unfairly judged by other nations. A lot could be said about how such an outcome might've also been the occasion for a *righteous-reset*, but it didn't happen. Instead, what could've been the opportunity for upscaling the national character, resulted the opposite: the birth of the National Socialist's movement. We know them as the *Nazis*. They single-handedly lit the match on the second World War, a blood-orgy that cost the planet 50-million lives.

16:20
It's a huge subject, how the great traditions of Germany and its **brilliant people fell victim to such a virulent form of self-pity,** but the part I found most intriguing was the flash-point known as *Blut und Boden*, an idea advanced by Nazi agriculturist, Richard Darré. The words translate: *blood* and *soil*. Germany needed space to grow it's crippled industry, as well as expanded access to much-needed resources. After years of humiliation and confinement, the Nazis were prepared to do whatever it took to establish a 1,000-year Reich, even if it meant stealing lands and soil that didn't belong to them.

17:05
The other component in Nazi sensibility was **the appeal to blood: racist-code for race-purity.**

God's people were the targets here. Keep in mind, ancient Israel practiced a form of race purity through regulated marriage. Jewish men married Jewish women. Consorting outside the ranks of Israel's sons and daughters was not encouraged. Why? Looking ahead to the birth of Messiah, perhaps God was amplifying, or protecting certain traits in Israel's gene pool. Jewish blood carried the promise of God's Son, whose shed blood, in due course, became the atonement for sin. The notion of **blood and sacrifice were massively important to Israel.**

17:55
The Nazis, by contrast, were attuned to an anti-Jewish bloodline. Rabid Nazi-evangelists proclaimed Jews an inferior race, whose intermarriage with the *Aryan god-race*, in ancient times, polluted the genetics. Israel conserved the lineage to Messiah. The Nazis sought to purge the lineage from which Messiah was drawn.

Perhaps it's too simplistic to suggest that Hitler and company were being puppeteered by a dark hand, but they certainly seemed to have been complicit in a cosmic game of blood-tag.

18:34
At the end of World War II, as the horror of the concentration camps became fully known, the world had compassion for the Jews. Why should they be exiled to nations that didn't want them? **In 1948, after nearly 2,000-years, the nation of Israel reappeared on the eastern coast of the Mediterranean, a reappearance heralded by the prophet Ezekiel in the 5th century BC, roughly 2,500-years before the fact.**

LifePlanning Notes – Journal

19:02
"... This is what the Sovereign Lord says: I will take the Israelites out of the nations where they have gone. I will gather them from all around and bring them back into their own land. I will make them one nation in the land, on the mountains of Israel. There will be one king over all of them and they will never again be two nations, or be divided into two kingdoms." (Ezekiel 37:21-22, NIV)

What began in the shedding of innocent Jewish blood in the 20th century, ended in unintended consequence.

19:38
Unintended Consequence
The Nazi will for blut und boden had the unexpected outcome of soil and blood, but for Israel. You could read it this way: God's plan is huge. **Satan exerts influence on human will, but the resulting sum has little impact on God's plan,** and may actually end up as a stark testimonial to Heavenly authority.

But couldn't God have given Israel soil, without the blood? This seems like a valid question, but it undershoots reality.

Evil happens. **Until God's plan eradicates evil – and that is part of God's plan – until then, He allows freedom for His children.**

20:24
When we feel that the **enemy is thwarting our advance to what God wants us to do in life, we're probably right.** The incredible reality is, if we pursue God's will for character, we're forced to a closer walk with the Heavenly Father. We're subsequently improved by Satan's opposition. The poor villain. **Another unintended consequence.**

20:48
When Paul tells us to *persist against adversity*, when James tells us *to resist the Enemy*, their counsel suggests that God continues with His unchanging plan. **Our responsibility is to remain confident in the Heavenly Father.** Eventually, Satan will probably be forced to give up on us for a season, at least. Those who persist in the faith are a huge drain on his resources. He may be powerful, but when he concludes that we're not worth the effort, **God's plan finds a way.**

21:24
The Mercy of the Lord
When I hear of a child who's been abused, or murdered, I tend to sink into depression. The older I get, the darker this reality seems to be. But somewhere along the line it hits me: **there's a point when the Heavenly Father says, Enough! He blesses the child, who blinks an eye in pain, earthside, then blinks again to discover God's comfort.** When you read the accounts of those who've had a near-death experience, many of them report a sudden, incredible peace, a fulfillment and relief when they cross over. **So much for the permanence of evil; such, is the mercy of the Lord.**

22:13
The Enemy may shadow our every move, but there's a point: God plan will be done. **Our responsibility is to craft character according to God's specification,** so that we can enter His plan with our love, showing.

When we understand: **God's will for our lives holds its target on character, we're liberated from the pressure of guessing at the future, or wasting time with pop metaphysics.** We're liberated to use our brains, with respect to vocation. *Love the Lord* *with all your heat, mind, soul and body.* The word *mind* is there.

22:55

A life in communion with the Heavenly Father has a lot of latitude in decision making. This is an attribute of God's mercy. The enemy will block you at every turn. Count on it. But ultimately, he's limited. As you yield to God, the more, you resist the enemy, the less attractive you are to him. 'Resist him and he will run away.' James 4:7

23:22

The evil-one **faces huge, unintended consequence when he trips you up. Imagine his chagrin when he tries to take you down, only to stand-by and watch you tumble up**, into the arms of a loving Heavenly Father. And perhaps, a new, even **better** job.

3
WHAT DID YOUR ANCESTORS KNOW?

LifePlanning Notes – Journal

There's an interesting chapter in the Bible. It's one I tend to avoid: Ecclesiastes 1:1-18. It was written by David's son, King Solomon; the narrative laments the futility of everything: life, work, wisdom, the ponderous, unrelenting course-of-nature. One of the most remembered verses in the chapter is the world-weary: *there's nothing new under the sun.*

00:33
You can't put a pretty face on this bit of prose. The interesting speculation is that it was written in old age. I buy that. What's especially curious is how my view of the chapter changed over the decades. As a young man, I didn't understand it. My best take was, *some old ancient guy was evidentially having a bad day.* Now that I'm something of an old, ancient guy myself, with more than a few bad days to show for it, I have an enlightened sense for what Solomon was talking about. Empathy aside, it's still **one of the most depressing chapters in the Bible.**

01:15
Solomon says, *one generation comes and goes and another takes its place, but the earth goes on forever.* **A few sentences later he says,** *everything requires labor.* Little consolation, to be reminded that our predicaments are not new, and our work, inevitable. We have a first bed. We have a last bed. Sometimes, as in the case of Christ, no bed at all.

01:44
The old king basically suggests that a lot of what we pour our lives into may not endure. Burial shrouds have no pockets for fame, fortune, influence, or power. Perhaps an argument could be made that character is the one thing we do take with us. If we are to be *known as we are known* in eternity. (1 Corinthians 13:12), I'd like to think that my better side would be showing, and everything else shoveled off into the sea of forgetfulness.

(Micah 7:18-19)

01:16
There's a marvelous scriptural balance to Ecclesiastes found in the New Testament. In the Sermon On the Mount (Matthew 5-7), Christ's words gently acknowledge Solomon's premise, but He picks up where the old king leaves off and completes the equation. Solomon reminds us of our lowly estate. Christ points us to *the Heavenly Father and a supreme spiritual inheritance.*

02:41
A Fistfight With Myself
A few years ago, Solomon's dark perspective got me thinking about my family, down through the ages. It started with a funny thought. What if a scientific breakthrough made it possible to go back and have a look-around at a world that used to be? My opening fantasy involved me, as a well-ripened old man, going back to visit myself as a green, highly-opinionated 18-year old. The more I thought about it, the funnier it got. I imagined a polite introduction to *young-me,* probably at a coffee shop, followed by *young-me's* disbelief at what he would eventually turn into. Near the end of the conversation, *old-me* would probably offer counsel for how *young-me* should live. The **cosmic encounter would thus end in a fistfight between** *me* and *me.* I say this on account of, when I was a young man, I was fairly offensive; as a old-man, I am probably mostly offensive, or so I'm told. The *young-me* would hate *my old-me* counsel; *old-me* would despise the *young-me's* arrogance. This little exercise told me a lot about myself, and the truth about my emerging character.

04:01
Expanding the fantasy a bit, **what if we could go back and visit all of our ancestors?** What would we discover? Themes, probably. We would find ancestors with physical characteristics like

our own. **We would find great grandparents, aunts, uncles, and cousins with interests-in-common, along with similar personality traits**. While the cultural differences would be significant, our forbearers endured their own encounters with LifePlanning. How would they recall the realities of survival and character?

Perhaps they'd warn against getting too smug. **Just when you think you've got it all figured out, something comes up, totally unexpected**. Life always surprises.

04:51
Another possibility. They might tell us: when you're young, you're strong, but stupid; when you're old, you're weak, but smart. This might be followed by another warning: **Don't get so caught up in the magic of the future that you overlook the magic that surrounds you, today**.

05:13
They would most likely echo Solomon's suggestion that we make the same mistakes, over and over. For the young, there's always impatience with the status quo, the practice of old method, archaic counsel, and unexamined procedure. With the old, there's always impatience with pointless change, unexamined counsel, the tendency to form over substance, and reckless procedure. **Hundreds of years ago, the generational seams might have been more subtle than today, but they were there**. The human family, after all, doesn't change.

05:50
One of the other topics our ancestors might bring up would be the recursive patterns of expectation, physical disaster, social bruising, family squabbles, raw ambition, competition, ruthless competition, disappointment – need we go on? Over the course of life, a lot of things happen to us. Back there, hidden in the

mists of the past, there's a pretty good chance, **someone in our family experienced the rough equivalent of what we've experienced.**

06:27

Two Classes

On our journey to the past we would probably discover two classifications of relatives. One, born with **an inkling of what they were supposed to do in life**, folks who sensed a general direction from day-one, then headed out with confidence. In this group would be all those whose vocations centered on traditions, practiced by their parents and grandparents. The children of blacksmiths, became blacksmiths; seamstresses begat seamstresses; bakers begat bakers. Also in this group would be visionaries, relatives who chased something on the horizon – the creatives, the inventors, and opportunists. Significantly, God's visionaries are found in this class as well.

If there's a downside to knowing what you're supposed to do in life, it's **the easy-vanity that comes with feeling superior to everyone else,** who doesn't.

07:29

The other class of ancestors would include **those who didn't have a specific direction for their lives.** They were a sturdy bunch, attuned to reason and opportunity. This group surveyed the options, sighted-in a vocational target, then came up with a game-plan. They didn't feel that they had been promised a particular result. There are a couple of unwelcome possibilities that often show up with this group. First, is **the vanity suggesting that we can design the future through good planning.** While it never hurts to have a solid idea for how to proceed, the reality is, the future is largely beyond our control. Our challenge is to be bright, methodical, and live humbly before the Lord.

08:17
The other downside for those who don't know, is the sense that they're second-class citizens. **Self-pity and resentment can really warp our personalities when we're constantly comparing ourselves to others.**

Curiously, some of our ancestors switched classifications over the course of a lifetime. Perhaps they were on a mission in the beginning, but arrived at a point where they had no specific direction to follow. Or conversely, had no particular sense of direction in the beginning, but eventually found themselves swept up in a mission. Life always surprises.

08:58
The Rich and Poor
Some of our ancestors were poor. Meagre circumstance confronted them with flash-points for character on a daily basis. Considering the indignities that often accompany poverty, perhaps they came to view it as a weird resource, and mined it for character. Poverty can turn us into a thief. Alternately, it can turn us into a spiritual-billionaire. **What we become in life is the direct result of what we permit ourselves to become.** Through God's counsel and blessing, we can achieve astonishing wealth, **yet remain poor in a temporal sense.**

09:43
Earth-side wealth, though, comes with its own troubles. For a few of our ancestors, having great riches alleviated some of life's challenges, but the big problems remained. An ample bank account didn't insure health, or the survival of beloved children. Our wealthy ancestors were blessed if they grew godly-character in the shadows of temporal security. **The wealthy run the greater risk of buying real estate on earth, when they should be**

laying up treasures in Heaven. (See Matthew 6:20)

10:17
Witness to Cosmic Reality
My guess is, after interviewing a few hundred of our long-departed ancestors, the godly among them would offer a fairly unexpected suggestion. Sometimes, **God reveals purpose through inclination or understanding.** We see a need, through the use of an ordinary set of eyeballs, can't get it off our minds, and proceed to make a difference. God might thus call us to noble service in just such a manner: through ordinary eyeballs.

There are also, what can only be classified as *God-calls*. Joseph was visited by an angel in a dream and told to take Mary as His wife. (Matthew 1:18-25) Saul was converted to belief in Christ through a vision on the road to Damascus. (Acts 9:3-9) The child Samuel heard a voice, whispering in the night. (1 Samuel 3:1-21)

11:27
Angels, visions, dreams, the voice of the Lord, all are mechanisms of LifePlanning, found in scripture. One of the most intriguing happened on the Mount of Transfiguration. It's recorded in both Matthew and Luke (Matthew 17:1-13, Luke 9:27-36), Christ and three disciples went up into a mountain where the glory of the Lord radiated from Christ like the sun. Moses and Elijah also appeared with Jesus, men who'd been dead for hundreds of years. It was an astonishing event.

Why did Christ invite only three of His apostles to this supernatural revelation, and not all twelve? **Why doesn't God give us all a vision for direction?** Or is this just another example of God playing favorites? Such questions will probably be fully understood from the shores of eternity, but Dr. George Wood offered a rather interesting, if not sobering, observation.

12:33
He said, **He'd always wanted to have a sign from God for what he was supposed to do in life.** That is, until he realized: supernatural revelations were almost always linked to trouble. **The person who experienced a special revelation from God inevitably faced a turbulent set of circumstances. That supernatural vision from an earlier time would be needed as a ballast for faith.** Dr. Wood made a further observation. Even in revelation, God never forces us to abandon freedom-of-choice, nor does He disengage the requirement for faith. What this means is: **even when we believe that God has spoken with great clarity, He never erases all questions. He never removes the tough circumstances that press us to cry out to Him, for Fathering.**

13:28
Revelation and Circumspection
There's an implication in the Transfiguration-account. The three apostles were probably numb-struck by the event; even so, the Lord told them to keep quiet about it until after His resurrection. (Matthew 17:9)

But why?

First, God's over-arching game plan – that all shall be saved – is played across space and time. Though the apostles might have been ready to announce God's cosmic revelation, the greater worth of the report would be achieved at an appointed hour. The other disciples would hear about the event, when God's plan would be better served. Then, of course, there's also the *Joseph-factor.*

14:19
The book of Genesis provides the account of a young man named Joseph. Not only was he beloved by his father, he was the recipient of dreams and visions, and he spoke of them, regularly.

The evidence suggests that Joseph's favor, along with his visions of the future, stirred up his brothers against him. **When God gives us a revelation, He might want us to hide it in our hearts for good reason.** Had He wanted to share that vision with others, He would have. He certainly doesn't give us a window of revelation to give us bragging rights. Quite the opposite.

14:56
The counsel of our godly-ancestors would probably follow along the lines of: *when God does reveal something to you, act on the revelation, but don't revel in it to others. Shut up and proceed. Get on with God's business.*

15:13
Character Endures
We can't go back in time and harvest the wisdom of our ancestors, but our elders are our closest link to that wisdom. In their counsel we discover: wisdom-of-age favors character.

While it's never safe to generalize, our ancestors would probably tell us how important friendships are, to our lives. Developing and keeping friends has a great deal to do with character.

Understanding how fragile life can be, and how fortunes can reverse in an instant, makes us more sympathetic and understanding with others. **Empathy has a great deal to do with character.**

15:58
Generosity **has to do with character.** Clear judgment **is related**

LifePlanning Notes – Journal

to character. Compassion has a lot to do with character. The motivation to console the grieving, has to do with character. Patience is rooted in character. Forgiveness has to do with character. The best of what we can be is rooted in character. And that simple pattern tells us something about ourselves and God's expectations for us.

It's really only a guess, an educated guess, but if your ancestors could speak, they might offer a list of LifePlan realities.

16:36

> *There are blind curves coming at you*
> *Some circumstances will change your life forever*
> *You'll have good days; you'll have bad days; you'll make*
> > *mistakes*
> *Sickness and injury will intrude on your plans*
> *You will misjudge others; you will be misjudged by others*
> *Trouble is inevitable; you will hurt and be hurt by others*
> *Death is inevitable*

17:08
To this list our God-serving ancestor might also add:

> *When godly character is the basis for LifePlanning, you*
> > *have a resilience that is not your own*
> *Christ's mission to Earth was to defeat our most obvi-*
> > *ous villain: death*
> *Through Christ, our eternal LifePlan succeeds*

4
SANTAfication

LifePlanning Notes – Journal

Pride

There's a naughty gravity about life that conspires against us. In Matthew 6:20, Jesus tells us to *lay up treasures in Heaven*, which makes a lot of sense. Loving God, living humbly before Him, with generosity and good will to all, are actually investments in eternity. And of course, when you practice this lifestyle, it **brings favor to your life.** C.S. Lewis described it like this. *Aim at heaven and you will get earth thrown in. Aim at earth and you get neither.* (Mere Christianity, Chapter 10)

00:41

For a time, I thought the secret to LifePlanning lay in starting at the right spot, vocationally. If I could just find that spot, the natural order of events should then proceed to convey me to destiny, without a lot of additional tending on my part. I could work at being a good man, get on with business, and with the time left over, focus on helping others.

I think my plot failed on two counts. First, there was no such thing as a *perfect* starting spot. Work is work. **Outcomes are unpredictable.** At some point, our investments may, or may not, bear the intended results. Second, a God-honoring life is not lived in isolation. Aiming at Heaven involves character, first, then connection to others. Maybe that connection takes the form of intercessory prayer, or empathy, or encouragement; maybe it takes the form of cold, hard cash. When we aim at Heaven, laying up treasures there, we become Heaven's paymaster on earth.

01:52

In the ebb and flow of reality, though, most of us have a tendency to drift off-target. **And one of the culprits in this gravitational tug, is pride.**

Without making a hard-fast indictment, it's fairly safe to say that most of us grew up being taught to *have a little pride* and *make something of ourselves.* This counsel was offered with good intention, no doubt, but once the sensibility was installed in our LifePlan, it turned into a nasty gravity. In Mere Christianity, C.S. Lewis suggested that **through pride, the devil cures your cold to give you cancer.**

02:31
Quoting from chapter 8:

"It is a terrible thing that the worst of all vices can smuggle itself into the very centre of our religious life. But you can see why. … Teachers, in fact, often appeal to a boy's Pride, or, as they call it, his self-respect, to make him behave decently: many a man has overcome cowardice, or lust, or ill-temper, by learning to think that they are beneath his dignity, that is, by Pride. The devil laughs. He is perfectly content to see you becoming chaste and brave and self-controlled provided, all the time, he is setting up in you the *Dictatorship of Pride*, just as he would be quite content to see your chilbains cured if he was allowed, in return, to give you cancer. For Pride is spiritual cancer: it eats up the very possibility of love, or contentment, or even common sense." (Mere Christianity, Chapter 8)

03:37
Notice that Lewis doesn't address LifePlanning in this passage, but it doesn't do a lot of damage to his intention, to pencil it in somewhere. Perhaps, along the lines: *The devil … is perfectly content to see you becoming chaste and brave, self-controlled and vocationally secure as he is setting you up in the Dictatorship of Pride.*

The blunt truth is: pride will sink your LifePlan. The nasty reality is: pride never shows up as pride. **It hides in the clutter of standards and practices, dresses up as a legal form of dignity, and pretends to represent higher values.** To continue in our rewriting of C.S. Lewis, he might have also said: *where character aims at Heaven, pride aims at earth.*

04:33
By the time we're plotting the course for where we're going to go when we grow up, pride is already in the wheel-house trying to steer. Early in LifePlanning, **pride attempts to influence our choice of vocation**; pride wants to assist us in finding something worthy of our gifts. Later, pride encourages our schemes-of-advance, steering us in the direction of shortcuts, and through anything and anyone that might accidentally be in our way.

05:06
When we suddenly lose our job, pride is often one of the first voices heard. It doesn't call us to a higher reconnaissance of our life, **pride grieves for lost status and wounded ego.** Chances are, since we're human, pride will never be completely defeated in our lifetime. Only, after our lifetime.

It might not be a bad idea to strive for a little objectivity on the subject. If pride is such a sneaky gravity, perhaps we do well to plot out its force field across our lives. An honest evaluation of what motivates us might reveal that **pride sits invisibly, at the center of our LifePlan, where it functions with all the gravitational subtlety of a black-hole.**

Pride tends to short-circuit our character development through a process of gradual seduction. It also warps our passage to Heaven.

06:07
SANTAfication
After pride, there's a second gravitational field that messes with my LifePlan.

God's ways will always be a mystery, but the ways of Santa are easy to understand. If I'm good, I get a toy. If I'm bad, I get a lump of coal. A fairly simple transaction. My problem with God, compared to Santa, is two-fold. First, He doesn't always indulge me with the bright and shiny plastic stuff I want. He gives better gifts than that. Second, seeking God means, I have to trust His ways. At times in my life, that's been a big problem.

06:51
I made up a word for my special gravity. I call it: *SANTAfication.* It's is not in the dictionary, but it hints at my misguided inclination for **confusing God with Santa Claus, and my material wish-list for God's will.**

07:08
After leaving Egypt, the Israelites grumbled about God's ability to provide for their needs. This is found in Exodus, chapter16. The Heavenly Father responded by sending down bread from Heaven, called *manna.* There was only one requirement. The Israelites could only take what they needed for the day. Should they try to store God's provision, or hoard it, the manna spoiled and turned wormy.

07:35
It became **an occasion for teaching Israel to trust God.** Undoubtedly, they understood the reasonable practice of saving for a rainy day, but with manna, they also learned: **they weren't to let hoarding replace their reliance on the Heavenly Father.** In LifePlanning, SANTAfication rears its ugly head when we take

up our cause as if there is no God, as if we must supply all our needs according to our riches on earth. Check out the book of Philippians, chapter 4:19, for a rebuttal on this point.

08:14
SANTAfication draws its course according to material obsession. **SANTAfication is the practiced-begging for trinkets and toys. SANTAfication meditates on giving in order to get. SANTA fication takes no shame in greed, excess or indulgence.**

And while we're at it, the list doesn't stop there.

08:38
SANTAchurch satisfies religious impulse. SANTAdeity conjures an easy atheist. SANTAdoctrine is enforced by a lump of coal. SANTAconfession happens in the lap of false promise (no kneeling required). **SANTAfaith expects more than daily mana.**

09:02
Trusting God for our daily bread may seem horribly naive and/ or irresponsible. To be honest, it would be easier to skip this point if Christ hadn't featured it so prominently in the Lord's Prayer: ... give us this day our daily bread. His intention couldn't be clearer. We are to acknowledge the providence of God; **we are to trust Him with our lives.**

In the passage from Matthew 6:19-21, Christ puts it bluntly. "Do not store up for yourselves treasures on earth, where moth and rust destroy, and where thieves break in and steal. But store up treasure in heaven, where moth and rust do not destroy, and where thieves do not break in and steal. For where your treasure is, there your heart will be also." (NIV)

09:55
Think of God's many gifts. He gives us partners in love. He gives children. Grandchildren. Beautiful little lights in a dark cosmos. He gives friendship, brothers, and sisters, whose pain and fortune become our own. He gives beautiful days and holy nights. Solitude and fellowship. Seasons. Memories that self-heal. In all of our wisdom, would we have had the intuition to pursue such wealth, according to our own design? **We have a rich Heavenly Father, with a genius for gifts. We can trust Him.**

10:36
Sadly, so much of our focus shifts to a mythical elf who indulges us with gifts of tinsel and shiny plastic. The lesson of trust, specifically: the willingness to suspend the wisdom of an earthly mind, in favor of a Heavenly mind, lies at the heart of godly character.

10:57
Dangerous Gravities/Breaking Free
It's not unusual to discover that **while we weren't paying attention, the gravitational fields that surround our LifePlan have warped our course.** I'm disgusted at how quickly I take up my own cause; I'm haunted at how effortlessly my default setting nudges out my fragile trust in a loving Creator.

Can we break free? Sure. In the Bible, people reset their Life-Plans on a regular basis. For example, have we done stupid things? A man named Saul, in the book of Acts, persecuted innocent Christian-believers. Then he had an encounter with the resurrected Christ. Saul reset his LifePlan and even had his name reset to Paul. He became one of the great writers of the New Testament.

LifePlanning Notes – Journal

11:49

Have we been knocked off course by the death of a loved one? **How do we proceed after great loss?** In the book of Ruth, a woman lost her husband. She had no prospects, whatsoever. But Ruth reset her life and discovered a new LifePlan.

12:06

Are we ashamed of our spiritual heritage? Do we lack nerve in the face of challenge? In the book of Esther, the Queen faced a test of courage, and won a huge victory for herself and ancient Israel. She had a reset in her LifePlan.

Trusting God **is the characteristic, common to all resets in Life-Planning**. It doesn't matter how you charted the course in the beginning, it's not too late to reset it, now.

5
Lands You Do Not Know

LifePlanning Notes – Journal

If you and God happen to be having coffee next Saturday, going over *next steps*, how will He respond to your big plan? **Does having a map for your life imply a lack of faith? Does not having a map imply a lack of industry?**

00:20

What makes the question intriguing, **the Bible shows an amazing amount of flexibility on this subject.** It seems to suggest that while it's legal TO HAVE a plan for what we're going to do, the reverse is also true. It's also legal, NOT TO HAVE a plan. Let's track through a quick list of examples.

00:39

People With No Plan

> *Adam and Eve's son, Abel, didn't plan to be murdered*
> *Abraham didn't plan to launch a trans-epochal enmity*
> *between Jews and Arabs*
> *Samuel didn't plan to have creepy sons who resembled*
> *the sons of his predecessor, Eli*
> *David didn't plan to kill Goliath, then eventually be-*
> *come Israel's king*
> *Peter had no initial plans to become the rock on which*
> *Christ's church was to be built*
> *Stephen didn't plan to be stoned to death*
> *Paul had no plan to become a believer in Jesus Christ*
> *John had no plan to die in exile on the isle of Patmos*

01:25

People Who Did Have A Plan

Actually, I'm not sure, I consider him a person, but, Satan does have plans to interfere with God's creation.

Among the more notable examples:

> *Noah had a plan for a massive boat*
> *Jonah had plans for avoiding what he'd been told to do,*

LifePlanning Notes – Journal

by God
Joseph had plans to safeguard Egypt during the years
        of famine
David had plans to build the Temple of the Lord
After exile, Israel planned to rebuild the temple of the
        Lord
Christ planned to do the will of His Father, in Heaven
The early Christian church planned to send out mission-
        aries
Paul planned to persist in his Christian faith until the
        end

02:15

Sometimes, we proceed without knowing what the next step is going to be. It's a concession to reality. We can't predict the future. On the other side of the coin, there are things about the future we do see. And when we do, we're in position to puzzle out a plan. Trusting God is the key in either case.

Admittedly, it isn't as simple a distinction as we'd like, but on-balance, **scripture emphasizes the rule-of-character in the matter of LifePlanning.** The book of James in the New Testament states it about as clearly as can be stated.

02:55

"Come now, you who say: 'Today or tomorrow we shall go into this or that city, spend a year and engage in business and make a profit.' Yet you do not know what your life will be like tomorrow. You are just a vapor that appears for a little while and then vanishes away. Instead, you ought to say, 'If the Lord wills, we will live and do this or that.' But as it is, you boast in your arrogance, all such boasting is evil. Therefore, to one who knows the right thing to do and does not do it, to him it is a sin." (James 4:13-17, NASB)

03:36
The passage implies that **planning isn't as big a deal as the context of your living.**

Perhaps the most important signal is the one that warns against arrogance and boasting. What are these attributes? Quite simply, they're issues of pride, and **pride short-circuits character.**

03:56
Abraham Hits the Road
Early-on, as I darted through the Bible, trying to sort out *what I was going to be when I grew up*, I bumped into the curious example of Abraham. The Great Creator saw something special in this man. Abraham was selected to be the Father of a great nation. We read about Abraham in Genesis 12:1-20.

In addition, God:
> *Promised to bless Abraham*
> *Declared His intention to protect Abraham*
> *Vowed to bless the human family, as a whole, through*
>   *Abraham*

04:35
The only problem Abraham faced: God withheld the specifics for how and when these things would transpire. In fact, his venture into **God's promise began with an unmapped first step: God told Abraham to** *go to a land he didn't know.* God would reveal the destination. (Genesis 12:1)

Sometimes, God's plan transpires in the absence of our own. Not knowing, but trusting God anyway, is something His people have practiced since time began.

05:13

Voodoo Christianity often advances the rather flaky notion that when you're in God's will, you'll experience complete liberation from trouble. We know this is both **goofy and a lie**; we see the truth-of-the-matter in the life of Abraham. When he jumped into the slipstream, heading for the future, Abraham did eventually make it to the land of God's promise; but then, something unexpected happened. He was led into the wilderness. He faced a famine, then war. We would like to think that God's highest, best use for us is that we retire. In reality, God sends us to places on the map where He expects us to go to work. Abraham fought a war, slipped into a treacherous situation with the Egyptians, and made his share of serious mistakes, all after reaching God's appointed destination. **We can reach our destination and still mess up.**

06:15

The Fabric of God's Will – Seen

Of all the declarations made to Abraham, the one that meant the most to him involved the gift of children, specifically the promise of a male heir. This was an important milestone in his culture. For God, Abraham's descendants were the direct link to the promise He'd made to Adam and Eve in the Garden. **Messiah was to be slipped into Abraham's gene pool, hundreds of years downstream.**

Abraham couldn't have foreseen how it would all play out, nor the milestones that would define his family, Israel.

06:55

Much of their history would be rooted in the creation of a spiritual ramp from which planetary salvation would be launched. We see this in retrospect. **What Abraham was looking for, was a baby boy.** He and his wife, Sarah, were impatient for that part of the vow to be fulfilled.

07:16
Jumping ahead in the account, one of the most difficult passages
we find about Abraham's life, involved the sacrifice of Isaac, the
child who eventually fulfilled God's promise. **The event became
Abraham's most successful flash-point.** It also provides an
astonishing display of stagecraft. When we place the set-pieces
under the spotlight, we see God's artistry suspended across time.
(Genesis 22:1-19)

07:51
As the sacrificial knife was raised, as the child's life was about
to be terminated, God provided a substitute. A lamb. Abraham
trusted God's intention. (Genesis 22:2)

In Hebrews 11:19, the Apostle **Paul was later to remark that
Abraham ... considered that God was able even to** raise him
from the dead, from which, figuratively speaking, he did receive
him back. (ESV)

08:21
Isaac marks:

> *The beginning of the gene pool that leads to Messiah*
> *The somber valuation of sacrifice*
> *A trail that leads to the crucifixion of God's Son*

08:34
Through Abraham's faith, God pulled back the curtain to reveal
the classical unities of mercy. We also project downstream, when
**another son, Jesus Christ, would become the lamb-of-sacrifice
several hundred years later. Abraham and Isaac provided the
pattern that would define God and His Son.** Our flash-points

of character could thus be said to hold great consequence. In the end, Abraham didn't sacrifice Isaac. He had faith in God's intention. By contrast, God did allow His Son to be sacrificed. And Christ was raised from the dead. There's mind-boggling resonance in God's ways.

09:20
Helping God Help Us
The interrupted sacrifice of Isaac marks a high point in Abraham's life. There were also low points.

Abraham and Sarah's greatest mistake took place well-before Isaac's birth, in the dark days when they were waiting for God to deliver on the promised baby. Sarah decided it was time to help God out. Working her way through a massive tangle of emotions, probably, she offered her servant, Hagar, to Abraham, for the reproductive services she was apparently unable to fulfill. It was a not-so-subtle suggestion that *God wasn't on His game.* (Genesis 16 and 21)

10:05
The account is well-worth reading. By the time Sarah gave birth to Isaac, there were two children in the house: **her child, representing the promise of God, and the other, representing an attempt to remedy what appeared to be the shortcomings of God.** Standard to the account were the inevitable jealousies between Sarah and Hagar, and the rising tension between Ishmael – Hagar's son – and his half-brother, Isaac.

10:34
When you've read the story, the slow-dawning reality is that while Isaac was the ancestor for Israel, Ishmael became the father for the Arab bloodline. Both populations share a direct ancestry in Abraham. The tension that existed between two

half-brothers is still played out in blood and fury in the mid-east.

Maybe this is an all-too-easy shot at Abraham, but it's true. This is the sort of thing that happens when **we concede character** and sidestep trust in the Heavenly Father. **We fall victim to unintended consequences of the darkest sort.**

11:14
Israel Had A Map
If Abraham lacked a map, several hundred years later, his descendants had a specific destination in mind when they departed Egypt. Under the leadership of Moses, they headed back to the land of Abraham's promise. To that end, they had something of a cosmic GPS system to get them there. During the day, they were led by a cloud. At night, they took their bearings from a pillar-of-fire. **To a spectacular degree:** Israel had a map.

According to the book of Deuteronomy, Israel's entire journey could've been accomplished in 11-days. Thanks to God's little GPS system, though, the sojourn took 40-years. How are we supposed to understand that?

12:04
Perhaps the most succinct answer is: **sometimes you can have the map, but lack the character.**

As we've chased the subject of LifePlanning, a couple of things kept showing up. First, as we've pointed out, God's will for us begins in our character, not in an external person, place, or thing. Second, an informed character is based on trust in God. It wouldn't be a total misreading of Israel's wilderness adventure to suggest that God's map for Israel contained **the additional landmark of national character.**

12:43

At the time of their departure, the Israelites were more than just slave laborers, they were **slaves of Egyptian custom, culture, ritual, and their own impatience.** If this newly emerging nation had one supreme character-flaw, it was disobedience. They were naughty on a regular basis.

But even though that's true, why would God allow an 11-day LifePlan to morph into one that takes 40-years?

13:16

Perhaps the long way is **one way to recalibrate faulty character.** Israel had seen the power of God in their escape through the Red Sea. They'd seen a spectacular manifestation of Him at Mount Sinai. They had witnessed His mercy through the provision of food and water. As His beneficiaries, God had expectations for their behavior. What their 40-years of wandering accomplished underscored the importance of character. Before they entered the land of promise, Moses' final words to Israel were blunt reminders of what they should've learned.

13:56

"And thou shalt remember all the ways which the LORD thy God hath led thee these forty years in the wilderness, to humble thee, and to prove thee, to know what was in thy heart, whether thou wouldst keep his commandments, or not. 8:3 And he humbled thee, and suffered thee to hunger, and fed thee with manna, which thou knewest not, neither did thy fathers know; that he might make thee know that man doth not live by bread only, but by every word that proceedeth out of the mouth of the LORD doth man live." (Deuteronomy 8:2-3, KJV)

14:35

A Not-So-Easy Confession

LifePlanning Notes – Journal

As I ran through the Biblical examples, tracking the list of planners and non-planners, I learned something about myself. I discovered that I gravitate to planning when I can see bits of the future. When this happens, character calls me to examine my motivations.

14:57
When I can't see the future, I'm a little more circumspect. Character calls me to wait on the Heavenly Father until the direction becomes clear. **The worst thing I'm tempted to do is throw myself at any and every possibility, without any discretion whatsoever.** Chasing all opportunities, without discretion, may satisfy my anxiety about the future, but it can be incredibly destructive to my LifePlan. It's a behavior that could possibly derail my investment in Heaven.

15:30
Prayer
We should bathe our plans for the future in prayer. (sermon, George O. Wood)

So many good things happen to our character when we humble ourselves before the Heavenly Father. So many problems are resolved. And the counsel to pray is not some kind of hokey call to mysticism, but a firm acknowledgement that we serve one, greater than ourselves. **The blanks in our plan are the spaces where God writes His love for us; the blanks in our plan are the spaces we practice our love for Him.**

6
HOW JESUS APPROACHED LIFEPLANNING

There are some basic questions that bring definition to our Life-Plan.

Who was Jesus Christ? is the first. This question defines a lot of history for the last 2,000-years. Today, people still celebrate Him in Europe, China, India, Africa, North and South America. **He's a trans-cultural, trans-epochal phenomenon.**

Why ... was He? The Great Creator **sent a representative of deity to enter a specific point in space and time.**

00:39
What was the reason for His coming? Jesus Christ **came to complete the connection from humankind to the dimension where the Heavenly Father dwells.** This connection took place on two levels.

First, the words of Christ revealed God's expectations. Second, Christ's sacrifice and resurrection created our **dimensional access-point** to eternity.

01:06
How is Jesus Proven? **Resurrection from the dead confirmed Christ's credentials.**

Eventually, we'll fully understand the breadth of Christ's mission, but for the moment, **all we have to do is believe on Him.** We don't have to fool around with talismans, send our life-savings to a televangelist, or solve all the great mysteries of the cosmos. The gift of salvation is an action-item that can be performed by the simplest, or the most sophisticated mind. That, in and of itself, is quite an accomplishment: *eternity, inclusion, divine love, and you don't have to take a math-test.* There's just one requirement. **Belief in Christ** is the first, and only order of business.

01:55
The Land of Suffering
For two-thousand years there have been discreet believers
who've read the histories, then quietly submitted to His Lord-
ship. Once past this simple threshold, **Christ sets up a living influence in a believer's life.** Through **daily communion** in prayer,
and the **reading of Holy Scripture**, Christ becomes a presence
on the order of a living friend or neighbor. But also, much more.
To understand Him on this level, one has to embrace Him as the
Son of God.

02:28
As we read about Jesus in Matthew, Mark, Luke, and John, we do
have questions about His earthly life. One of the biggest is: **how
much of Him was God, and how much of Him was human?**
Welcome to upper-division theology.

> *Did Christ have a LifePlan?*
> *How much did He know about what would happen next?*
> *Did He have it easier because He was also God?*

02:53
According to Paul: "Although He existed in the form of God,
He did not regard equality with God a thing to be grasped, but
emptied Himself, taking the form of a bond-servant, and being
made in the likeness of men." (Philippians 2:6-7, NASB)

03:12
Taken at face value, Paul's statement suggests that Jesus faced life
much the way the rest of us do. He endured pain. He engaged
the same questions and realities, we experience. And if the passage in Philippians isn't enough, there's the haunting statement
in Hebrews which should be written across every LifePlan. *Al-*

LifePlanning Notes – Journal

though he was a son, he learned obedience from what he suffered.
(Hebrews 5:8, NIV)

When you arrive in the land of suffering, you've also arrived in
the place where character is built.

03:47
The LifePlan of Christ
We don't know a lot about the early life of Christ. One account,
however, provides a revealing snapshot of how much He knew
about Himself, by age 12.

His family had journeyed to Jerusalem for Passover. (Luke
2:39-52) As they returned home, Mary and Joseph discovered
that Jesus wasn't part of the entourage. They turned around
and headed back to Jerusalem, where they found Him in the
Temple, in discourse with the teachers and elders. According
to Luke, the Temple professionals were amazed at His understanding.

04:23
Mary and Joseph were relieved to find Him, but also a little
upset, perhaps. Mary said something along the lines: What are
you doing? We've been worried about you.

Christ responded, *don't you know that I have to be about my
Father's business?*

04:40
With this response, Jesus sent a clear signal about the existence
of a LifePlan. In a voice, resonating with command, Christ-at-
twelve emphasized His commitment to my Father's business.
This was not an inadvertent poetic liberty. Jesus was saying
something that could've been considered blasphemous by the

very teachers with whom He was conversing. A cynic might further observe, He wasn't just recommending Himself to the ranks of deity, but offering a not-so-subtle dismissal of Joseph, the righteous man who had been His father, by adoption.

05:19

Note the two things taking place in this simple transaction. First, Jesus was reminding Mary and Joseph of what Heaven had already revealed to them. Of equal significance, Jesus was putting the teachers of the Temple on notice: *a boy, proclaiming Himself to be God's Son had landed in the neighborhood.* After this, Christ consigned Himself to His parents and returned to Nazareth. Luke added something of a postscript, commenting that *Jesus continued to increase in wisdom and in favor with God and man.*

05:55

Several issues of godly-character are apparent here. It's obvious, **Christ had a sense of where He was heading, early-on.** He demonstrated a lot of resolution for a 12-year old kid. Specific manifestations of character are also seen in His obedience to Mary and Joseph. Though He'd given them a dose of clarity, He didn't disgrace them, or disobey their request.

06:22

Finally, we have Luke's follow-up observation that Christ grew in favor with God and man. This is active proof of Christ's godly-character, in the making. As a young man, **Jesus was oriented to His Heavenly mission, but respectfully connected to His human family, as well.**

06:43

Timing, Timing, Timing
It's been said, the three most important things we need to know about real-estate are *location, location, location*. With a godly

Floyd Wray

LifePlanning Notes - Journal

LifePlan, the three most important things we need to remember are *timing, timing, timing.*

07:04
Our lives are cast across time. We have a beginning, a middle, and an end. When we're finally old enough to model the future, mentally, we start looking ahead to what happens next. This is normal. **As we've already pointed out, some of us have a strong sense for what we're supposed to do in life; the rest of us discover what we're supposed to do, like Abraham.** In both instances, what happens next, happens on a calendar. **Character also happens on a calendar.**

07:36
The year I graduated from high school, I was ready to proceed directly into my imagined destiny. But that's not the way it worked out. Until that point, I had been absolutely clueless on the subject of timing. I'm not sure whether this was due to native ignorance, or childish fantasy. Probably both. Looking back, of course, I see how **timing choreographed my LifePlan.**

08:02
> *Dad resigned his job and we moved to a new city, my*
> *senior year in high school*
> *I was seriously discouraged about leaving my childhood*
> *friends*
> *The first day at my new school was disgusting*
> *Then I made new friends and came to love my new school*
> *I met a beautiful girl at my new school*
> *We dated for a couple of years and got married*
> *We had a wonderful son, who married a beautiful girl*
> *I am now a grandfather with stunning grandchildren*

08:40
The day I left my old high school, my emotions were all over the

map. Obviously, I had no idea that a beautiful blonde was waiting for me at the other end of the transition. If I had seen her, or even suspected her existence, the move would've been cake. By such measure, we all move forward in life. **We step from unknowns to knowns, and back again.**

"To everything there is a season, and a time for every purpose under Heaven." (Ecclesiastes 3:1, KJV)

09:17
The Time Analogy
Timing is often easier to understand when you compare it to something that makes obvious use of it. Like music. In any given song, the musical narrative typically consists of notes, marking the melody. **Play them all at the same time and you achieve something on the order of a belch.** Place them in the right sequence, in a specifically-timed sequence, and you get music. Add several instruments, each with their own set of notes to play, and you have a fairly nice analogy for how timing makes a difference: how stuff has to show up at a specific point, in alignment with other stuff, that also shows up at the same, specific point.

10:03
There's another interesting analogy for timing. Those of us who see life as a game of checkers, see a two-dimensional game board defined by red and black squares, usually. These squares mark off width and length. The game is defined by these boundaries.

Checkers have a start point: your side of the board. There's also a plan. You set out to capture your opponent's checkers. In the end, the winner usually chases the loser around the board until the loser can run no more.

10:34

Chess is roughly the same game, with a few small distinctions. The game is also played inside a two-dimensional space. Action starts on one side of the board. As before, each player succeeds as they reduce the opponent's strength through the taking of game pieces. This is where you start to see the difference between chess and checkers. With chess, the various pieces have defined characteristics. Some pieces move one way, and only one way. Others are licensed to move in several directions, and manifest specific strength, or advantage.

11:13

With a little imagination, and a plexiglas frame, we can redraft the metaphor from two, to three-dimensional chess. And to be accurate, it would actually employ four dimensions. Chess, played across multiple levels, has height, width, depth, and time about it. **Four-dimensional chess requires a more intense strategy-of-alignment. Alignment is something that takes place in time.**

11:42

When we see our LifePlan as a game of checkers or chess, we're **focused on the next move.** God, though, sees the game board against the measure of eternity. Our tactical lesson from this analogy, underscores **the need for us to be persistent**, as we wait on the Lord and renew our strength. (See Isaiah 40:31)

Oh, one other thing. *Persistence* is an attribute of character.

12:14

An Unexpected Attribute of Timing

Christ knew about timing. Just before He launched His public ministry, the subject came up during a wedding-celebration. (John 2:1-11) Again, as before, His mother Mary was part of the conversation. In a bid to head off social embarrassment, Mary told Jesus, the wedding host was about to run out of wine. The implied request was: Is there anything you can do?

Again, Jesus displayed an incredible sense of His LifePlan. **He told her that *His time had not yet come*.** The response seemed to deflect her request; but then, He proceeded to honor it, and turned the water into wine.

12:59
Wait. What? If His time had not yet come, why did He concede the intervention? It's safe to say, part of His response was Jesus being Jesus. His miracle was in keeping with what we know about Him and His compassion.

But what if there was something else in-play?

13:21
It had been roughly 18-years since that day in the Temple with Mary. By this point, it's safe to assume, Christ had a more complete understanding of His mission. We aren't specifically told how much had been revealed to Him, but it's obvious, He knew a lot about time and eternity. He described Satan's fall from the Heavens. (Luke 10:18) We sense His familiarity with Moses and Elijah on the Mount of Transfiguration. (Mathew 17:1-13) **He knew about the past. He had strong intuitions about the future. He knew the seasons of His existence.**

3:57
If we experience both a sense of mission, as well as a sense of where our godly LifePlan is taking us, Christ probably experienced something of rough equivalence. From His vantage point, though, He saw past the curtain of timed-reality, into eternity. **He knew of the huge war raging there. He also modeled the**

LifePlanning Notes – Journal

implications of that war, and how the shrapnel of that conflict crashed through into the stream of human events.

14:27
Christ walked a tightrope between time and eternity. He held Himself in subjection. He also drew a line in the sand when God's eternal plan was threatened with compromise. At one point during His public ministry, **He would command evil spirits to stop acknowledging Him. They had no right to proclaim Him as the Son of God.** They were out in the cosmos, infesting and destroying innocent lives. They weren't worthy heralds, even as truth-tellers. **Christ was quick to guard His revelation, and the timing that staged His mission.**

15:06
At the wedding-celebration, though, Christ wasn't talking to evil spirits, He was talking to His mom. He seemed to be saying: mom, you aren't in charge of my revelation, you aren't the boss of me. After all these years, Christ was still committed to being about His Father's business, **deferring to Heaven's timetable.** Mary wasn't in charge of the *whats* and *whens*. Having administered another dose of clarity, though, Christ proceeded to turn water into wine.

Back at the Temple ... forward-in-time to the wedding ... **Christ revealed His commitment to a LifePlan, followed by respect and mercy.**

15:50
Big and Distant/Small and Near
Christ understood, His earthly behavior would impact generations yet to be born. He also had a sense of His immediate neighborhood. **This sets an interesting standard for our Life-Plan.**

Most of us have highly motivated friends who've set lofty goals for themselves, professionally. Some target educational milestones; some focus on professional achievement; some pursue hyper-vanity, disguised as a high and worthy cause. Sometimes, these highly motivated friends ... are US.

16:33

In The Bishop's Wife, with Cary Grant, David Niven, and Loretta Young, we see the story of a clergyman with a near-insane ambition to build a cathedral. Niven's character is **so blinded by his big and distant goal, he fails to see that he has practically abandoned his family, not to mention his increasingly marginalized friends.** It's a fairy tale, but one with teeth. According to the fiction, God sends Dudley-the-angel, played by Cary Grant, to help reawaken the Bishop's equally important sense- of-mission to the small and near.

17:12

As a side-note, I've always been of the opinion that The Bishop's Wife should be licensed, then shown, every time religious leaders get together for a conference. The presentation should be followed by **a time of repentance and prayer.**

17:29

As we focus on our big mission, there's a temptation to view the people around us as incidental, or even as a distraction. Eyes fixed on destiny, some of us get so focused on our big thing – out on the horizon – that **we stomp forward, across the fragile lives of our beloved family and friends.** There is a fine balance between working and trusting, between preparing for the future, and living in the present. Louis Pasteur once said: *chance favors the prepared mind.* To that it could be also said: *eternity favors the engaged and loving heart.*

18:13
When we imitate Christ, our LifePlan **includes the big and distant as well as the small and near.** What good are grand, cosmic schemes for destiny if they're based on the exile of local mercy?

18:29
Sketch Out A LifeMap
If I were to sketch out my LifeMap, the milestones would be represented by circles, one of which would be labeled: *godly communion*. There would be another circle for *family* and *friends*. I would also draw a circle labeled: *mission*.

18:47
There would be circles with a slightly odd labels, representing my own flash-points for character. A circle labeled Christ's eyes, for example. What does that mean? It's something I picked up over the years: a classification that represents my **intention to see the world the way Christ sees it.** This matters to me. Christ's eyes help me perceive an impoverished couple walking their 6-year old to school. Christ's eyes alert me to the physically impaired young man who staggers into my coffee shop every morning.

19:23
Christ's eyes challenge me to see old people, driving white Buicks at 5-mph in my lane, as beloved of God. When I view the world through Christ's eyes, **I'm alerted to take tangible action** on what they reveal to me. Christ's eyes are an intentional milestone on my map.

19:45
Sketching a LifePlan on paper provides a revealing visualization of who we are and where we're heading. While I favor a sketch

showing ideals as milestones, a map could just as easily be drawn to illustrate priorities.

20:01
For example, the primacy of one circle over another could be indicated by size or color. Simple stuff, really. But once we have a visualized map in place, it's a rather simple transaction to run an inventory, comparing our *hopeful* milestones with the bone-crushing reality of our daily schedule.

Should we attempt to map out timing on our map? This is a worthy question; it's also, a question we've touched. (See James 4:13-17)

20:37
LifePlan – A Few Annotations
When, or if, we attempt to map our LifePlan, we should include a few scriptures on the page somewhere. Mentioned previously, there's that great, but cautionary scripture in Hebrews 5:8: *Although he was a son, he learned obedience from what he suffered.* (NIV)

Another is found in Matthew 10:38: *Anyone who does not take up his cross and follow me is not worthy of me.* (NIV)

7
THREE ISSUES OF CHARACTER

Randy Newman wrote a song entitled, *I Just Want You To Hurt Like I Hurt.* Without getting into the song's narrative, just the title provides a tool for understanding. There are probably a million reasons for why God constructed our reality the way He did, but part of **His plan included hurting like we hurt.** Why would He do this? Had I been in charge, I would've invented something easier. I would've zapped out the pain, passed out no-calorie ice cream and chocolate, and decreed that everyone gets a pony. **Why does life have to be so hard?** Did God have to enter our reality to fully comprehend just how difficult human existence can be sometimes? **It should've been obvious from all the screaming.**

00:53
I can't fully answer this question, but I'm satisfied with a partial explanation. The Heavenly Father is known as the *Father of Lights.* His Son, Jesus Christ, is known as *the light of the world.* In the Father's illumination, we see eternal destiny. In His Son's illumination, we see the trail that takes us there. And **there is a cross in the middle of that trail.** The visibility of that cross puts us on notice.

01:28
Israel and Christ – In the Wilderness
I'm fairly convinced that both religious and non-religious bystanders miss the symmetries of God's amazing revelation. On both sides of the aisle, Christianity is often framed by clichés and stereotypes. The truth is, not only is scripture just plain fascinating to read, the closer you look, you **find repeating patterns that build and resonate, layer upon layer, as God reveals Himself.**

02:02
A good example is seen in the previous quote from Ezekiel,

LifePlanning Notes – Journal

37:21-22. The passage directly addresses the period following Israel's Babylonian captivity. But the scripture also attaches to an impressive list of passages that predict Israel's return as a nation, just prior to the end-times. Speaking of which, Israel joined the family of nations again, in 1948.

In **repetitive patterns, we see a strange coherence in the way God reveals Himself.**

02:39
Keeping this in mind, let's look at the tests of character that marked the beginning of Christ's ministry. After 40-days in the wilderness, a time spent in fasting and prayer, Christ was confronted by Satan.

02:54
Think about the patterns.

> *Israel wandered in the wilderness for 40-years. Christ was in the wilderness for 40-days.*
> *Moses revealed the covenant between God and Israel through the administration of law. Christ revealed the fulfilled the covenant between God and humanity through the administration of grace.*
> *Moses' message in Deuteronomy was delivered just before Israel entered into a new kingdom. Christ's call-back to that message was delivered just before He entered into public ministry, where He would proclaim the kingdom of God.*

03:36
After 40-days, not eating, Satan made an open appeal to Christ's physical hunger. Keep in mind, Jesus' exercise in fasting was attached to His spiritual passion. Satan thus affronted His commitment, **reducing it to a purely physical transaction.** He was

dismissing the spiritual component, completely.

03:58
Thinking back to Moses, the fear of hunger had provoked Israel into murmuring and complaining. But Israel didn't actually fail a hunger test, they failed the trust test. Christ passed. It was obvious, Jesus had studied the subject rather thoroughly. And here's the recursive part. He answered the Enemy with the words of Moses: *…man doth not live by bread only, but by every word that proceedeth out of the mouth of the LORD doth man live.* (Deuteronomy 8:3, KJV)

04:32
Was Satan **following something like a call-script here?** Maybe. As a strategy, he was making a direct appeal, using an approach that had worked in the past. But why would he trot it out again? **Was He testing the Lord's hunger, or His character?** In either case, Christ's answer from Deuteronomy slapped down the challenge in grand style.

04:55
Luke records the second temptation as Satan's offer to give Christ rule over the kingdoms of the earth. This is odd. The Sunday school answer is that Jesus already owned the neighborhood; He and His Heavenly Father were already in charge. Satan was lying, or maybe there was something else going on here.

05:16
Christ was destined to rule anyway, but falling down and worshipping Satan at this point, **would have been a lot quicker and easier than pursuing God's trail to blood-sacrifice.** Satan was calling Jesus to an easy ascendancy, but again, Christ told him, in no uncertain terms: *worship only the Lord your God.* It's a dark thought that **Jesus might've been chased off His mission**

by the mere promise of an easy workaround. Was He really at risk? No. Christ was perfectly oriented to reality. When the Enemy targets our possible weakness, we have to **measure quick rewards against those, eternal.** Christ did. He made the right decision.

06:02
Luke describes the third temptation. Christ was taken to the pinnacle of the Temple in Jerusalem, and challenged to *prove God*. This is the crudest temptation of all because it targets Christ's personal revelation. Satan must've believed there was vulnerability here. He challenged Christ to jump. If Jesus was who He said He was, God wouldn't allow Him to be injured.

06:28
This was the same Temple where young Jesus had been about His Father's business. Christ had a lot in common with those who hung out in that part of town. Sadly, in the end, He would be dismissed by them, and actually, worse than that, they would plot His death. **Satan thus offered a preemptive redress of a looming rejection and public embarrassment.** Jesus fully understood what the Enemy was offering.

Back in the days of Moses, Israel tested God, trying to manipulate Him. In this case, the enemy was giving **Christ the chance to call God out on His promises**: to manipulate God into validating Christ's credentials, publicly. Again, Christ quotes Deuteronomy. "You shall not tempt the Lord, your God." (Deuteronomy 6:16, ASV)

07:22
A lot has been written about Christ's temptation in the wilderness. Understanding what went down there, and the many connections between Israel's national character and Christ's, has

a lot to say about what we face. **So much of what we look for in a LifePlan focuses on temporal security, an easier lifestyle, recognition, and confirmation.** It's unfortunate that **our intense desire to capture these targets tends to yank us off-target.**

07:54
Been There Done That
Christ's temptation demonstrates a couple of important points. **First, His humanity was modeled into His LifePlan, not modeled apart from it. Second, the Enemy tested Him for weakness, pretty much the same way he tests us.**

08:13
From what little we know about Jesus in the quiet years, from age 13 to 30, we suspect, He was **doing the homework on character during that time.** The clues are found in passages like Luke 2:52, where we're told, *He grew in favor with God and man.* Another is found in Hebrews 5:8, which proclaims that *through His suffering, he learned obedience.* In Hebrews 4:15, the writer points out that *Christ endured what we must also endure.*

There's something unavoidable in this. The character of Christ was grown by challenge. What an amazing way to discover the future. By the time the Enemy took his best shots in the wilderness, Jesus had already addressed the issues. In fact, He'd even gone so far as to footnote them from the book of Deuteronomy. The engine-of-challenge that drives character prepared Christ for the assaults that would eventually show up in His LifePlan.

09:16
Growing character is not unlike growing an immune system. A child's body faces a dangerous situation in the beginning. Threatened by pathogens and tumor cells, the body can only resist such things through a complex process of detection and

neutralization. In an amazing act of design, the child's body actually adapts to pathogens over time, and progressively tunes this complex system, in terms of detection and defense. This is one of the reasons why we send children to daycare centers, so they can catch stuff from other kids and ... *what doesn't kill them, makes them stronger.*

09:59

Through a slight stretch of analogy, we can sketch out a comparison between a newborn, and the **spiritual viruses that a newborn-believer encounters as they discover what they want to be when they grow up.** Every time we find ourselves at a funeral service, or visiting a friend in the hospital, our LifePlan is exposed to the dark truth of the human condition. We get sick. We die. Sometimes, we die ... slowly. This is the top-level pathogen against which our LifePlan must prevail. And where's the vaccination for this condition? At the risk of being dismissed as too simplistic, **our vaccination was formulated at the cross where Christ absorbed the body-blow for sin and death.**

10:49

When we accept Christ's gift of salvation, we've taken the Master's inoculation against eternal death. Even so, we spend the rest of our earthly life **getting boosters.** Not for eternity, necessarily, that's already been cured, but as long as we walk the planet, **our godly character is under threat.** Progressively, as we succeed spiritually against flash-point after flash-point, **our auto-immune system builds resistance to those weaknesses that would otherwise take us down.** When Christ landed in the middle of Satan's challenge, He had taken all the necessary boosters.

11:29

So what's the worth of the troubled-reality we face? In a resonance that looks and acts like the human auto-immune system, it's another case of *what doesn't kill us only makes us stronger.* And if by some unexpected fluke it does actually kill us, in Christ's resurrection, we're covered there, too.

8

EXPECTATION

With children, expectation **is often a short fuse to a hissy.** Tell your granddaughter you're taking her to the park. A few minutes later, tell her, I changed my mind, let's stay at home. There's a fairly good chance your announcement will set off a conniption, or I don't know 2-year olds. Expectation screams large when it's violated. It comes in at least two, especially ruthless flavors: **one based on misdirected hope; the other, false targets.**

00:37
The best example of the former was seen in Israel's expectation for Messiah. Many people assumed he'd be a warrior like King David. They wanted a super-hero to kick out the Romans and restore Israel's ancient glory. For these folks, **Christ simply didn't live up to their expectation of what a Messiah should look like.**

00:59
Jesus, of course, was all about establishing the Kingdom of Heaven, not a kingdom on earth. And His profile was obvious. Long before His public ministry, Hannah and Simeon perceived His true identity as a newborn. (Luke 2:21-40) Once His ministry began, **Jesus was easily perceived by an honest heart and a normal set of eyes.**

01:26
I've often wondered, had I been alive in those days, would I have perceived Him, or would I have also suffered *expectation?* **Imagine how disconcerting it would be to discover, your fiction for Messiah distracted you from the fact that He was just a couple of blocks from your house at some point.** But that's one of the things it does. **Expectation can blind you.**

LifePlanning Notes – Journal

01:51
LifePlanning and Expectation
Most of us model our job-futures based on a variety of things.
We expect to start at the bottom, then work our way to the top.
We:

> *Plan to succeed because we expect to do the jobs no one*
> *else wants, in the beginning*
> *Carefully pick the right career moves*
> *Work long hours*

02:18
On this last point, some of us seem to think, **a willingness to
sacrifice family and friends for our job proves something**. The
ugly truth is, we can slave away, 24/7, only to have our boss kick
us to the curb for no good reason. In spite of our allegiance to
our jobs – and our expectations of mutual fidelity – our jobs
may have no allegiance to us.

02:45
Over the years, I've worked with several technology start-ups.
My bosses tended to be younger than I, and my peers a lot
smarter. But most of them bought into expectation and its atten-
dant mythologies. What can I say? **They were young.**

One of my favorite consultancies was with a small company,
staffed by an incredible group of young people. As the se-
nior-adult (I was maybe 36-years old at the time), **I was partic-
ularly impressed at the long hours they were willing to put in.**
They would arrive at work in the morning, bleary-eyed, and tell
me they'd been in the office past midnight. No one ever said it to
my face, they were too gracious, but I started to feel that I might
be letting everyone down by even heading home, at all, in the
afternoon. Of course, I had a beautiful wife and wonderful son
waiting for me. **They were more important to me than the job.**

03:43
Eventually, out of guilt, mostly, I did stay late a few nights. Imagine my surprise to discover that the work actually ground to a halt less than an hour after my normal time-of-departure; at which point, my colleagues pretty-much closed the books and sat around talking. Then someone brought in a six-pack, then someone else brought in another, then another, and another. Around 9:30 p.m., my young protégés began staggering out to their cars. There's an important distinction between working smart and working long. **The expectation that long hours automatically translate to success may not be true, if** long is also wrong.

04:31
Late-evenings aside, these young people were dedicated. They had big dreams. They were talented; in a couple of cases, brilliant. Even so, they worked **under the influence of a delusional expectation.** The company closed down a couple of years later. All the hours, whether real or fantasized, were thrown to the wind. The only monument to the effort was the memory of a great cause, and the sad reality that comes with divorce and career-restart. Expectation **is easily seduced by** delusion.

05:10
Self-inflicted Expectation
When you were little, you dreamed of being a super-hero. Older kids confirmed what you already suspected: the power of flight and manifestation of super-powers began with a good cape. So, you tied mom's towel around your neck, jumped off the garage, and broke both arms. Expectation, along with a few other lies, betrayed you. A good cape didn't rocket you into the sky; what it did was rocket your vocabulary to new definitions for *pain, convalescence,* and *aerodynamics.* And *crazy.*

LifePlanning Notes – Journal

05:54

Faulty expectation is often based on a lack-of-experience. Lying beneath the basketball goal, we curse the lies they tell about capes, and then ourselves for being so stupid.

Expectations always tend to be a bit faulty. Sometimes, we're not actually wounded, physically; sometimes, our emotions are bruised; sometimes, our dreams are tossed out with the trash. **In the wake of crash-landed expectation, we have a flash-point, a chance to see what's hidden in the dark corners of our aspiration.** As painful as the moment may be, lying face-down, cape fluttering stupidly in the breeze, we have a glorious chance to reset our sense-of-reality. You have to wonder how many airline pilots began their careers at the end of an otherwise non-functional cape.

06:58

My Friend Walter

If lack of experience accounts for some of our short-flights, fantasies and vain-imaginings account for most of the rest.

My last year in college, **the theater-critic for the New York Times, Walter Kerr, came to our campus for a lecture.** At the time, I had a fairly wide set of interests and expectations. I planned to be a writer, make movies, write plays, and most of all, explore the unknown space where technology and language share a common border. A space I'm still exploring, 40-years later.

07:39

After the lecture, I caught Mr. Kerr in the hall. I thanked him for his time, then asked the most prescient question my 20-year old mind could muster. I asked what effect new technologies – like the just-announced Laserdisc – would have on the theater.

LifePlanning Notes – Journal

Keep in mind, to know about such things, you had to be what passed for a nerd in those days. The Laserdisc was still out on the horizon, and wouldn't land on planet-earth for at least another 7-years or so. But my asking the question proved ... actually I'm not sure what it proved, now that I think about it. Maybe something along the lines of: **a penniless, sub-average college student, groping for self-worth, was mouthing off to an urbane, well-received man-of-the-world, telling him, in essence,** *well, I'm smart too.*

08:34

Mr. Kerr smiled, then responded as if he'd read the fuller context of my question, telling me that there were *incredible technologies on the horizon.* He couldn't wait for them to show up. He also said, technologies like Laserdisc would probably have *more impact on the film industry than the Broadway stage,* but *that young people, like you, have an amazing future ahead of you.*

08:53

What followed this brief encounter, hints at either **my potential for stupidity, or just how forlorn my prospects were at the time.** I walked away feeling fairly special that a well-known personality had even spoken with me. And by the time I got home, I'd convinced myself that I'd made a favorable impression. He must have concluded: *here's a young man, fully aware of what's really happening in the world.*

09:28

By the next morning, **my cheeks were still flushed with a sense-of-favor.** I imagined that Mr. Kerr walked away with the dean, and as they proceeded to the reception, perhaps he'd asked: *who was that brilliant young man?* By the next afternoon, my fantasy – expectation in tow – had concocted a scenario. Upon arriving back in New York, Mr. Kerr had called his staff in to tell them

LifePlanning Notes – Journal

about *this incredible young man I met yesterday. Harper and Putnam on the phone. Someone needs to sign this kid.*

10:05
Since the lecture had taken place on a Monday evening, I figured it was unreasonable to expect a call until Wednesday or Thursday, at the earliest. Until then, I'd have to be patient. Get all my files into boxes, fold my clothes. Make a few to-do lists. **I didn't like the idea of moving to New York, but sacrifices would have to be made.**

10:29
Aye-yi-yi. This simple string of expectations completely humiliates me today. Even though I have enough distance on the subject to offer it as an example, the memory still stings me. In student-desperation, my aching need for acceptance deposited me in the middle of an ever-expanding silliness. Needless to say, a month later, when Mr. Kerr's office had not called, and I hadn't heard anything from a major publisher, my heart crashed. The little fiction I'd allowed, as stupid as it was, had provided temporary relief from reality. Like a sugar-high, though, it was to provide no serious energy for my race, and left me completely demoralized.

Expectation is more than sugar, though, it can be a cruel narcotic. The best rehab is not to get hooked on it in the first place.

11:30
Targets
In addition to caped-flight, there's another interesting analogy for expectation. Some Christians think of God's will as an archery target, with a bull's-eye marking the center: *God's Perfect will.* After the bull's-eye, *Sorta' God's Will,* might be the name for the second ring; and *Barely, the third.*

Where did this idea originate? How did we ever conjure the notion that God's will promised 1st, 2nd, and 3rd place trophies? Perhaps it comes from a misreading of scripture.

12:12
"I beseech you therefore, brethren, by the mercies of God, that ye present your bodies a living sacrifice, holy, acceptable unto God, which is your reasonable service. And be not conformed to this world: but be ye transformed by the renewing of your mind, that ye may prove what is the good, and acceptable, and perfect, will of God." (Romans 12:1-2, KJV)

12:38
Many of us take this to mean, there are varying levels to God's will. Unpacking the verse, we might conclude: even if you just nick the target, you're in God's *permissive* will. Hit a little closer to the center, and you move up to the will of God. And if you're a super-Christian, you'll nail the bull's-eye. In his sermon, Dr. Wood made an important point: *Good, acceptable,* and *perfect* are synonyms, not levels.

God's will is always good, acceptable and perfect, he said. What else would it be?

13:21
In addition to the supporting scholarship, Dr. Wood's **synonyms offer us a heavy dose of common sense.** If there were scaled zones to our LifeTarget, we would be trapped in a manic game of connect-the-dots. Every choice would have a magic center-point representing God's milestone-to-destiny. Taken to the absurd, one missed milestone along the trail could result in a potentially disastrous re-routing of outcome; the choice of corned beef over grilled-cheese, for instance, could end in an unintended chain-of-events and the collapse of the Bolivian government.

LifePlanning Notes – Journal

If this smells like pop-metaphysics, it is. It's also silly.

14:11
We make mistakes. It's inevitable. And we suffer for our goofy choices. But here's where God's grace is even more astonishing. *All things will eventually work out for our good,* **no matter how stupid our career choices, as we humbly pursue a relationship with the Heavenly Father.** (Romans 8:28) God's will targets our relationship with Heaven, first and foremost. **Not our earthly ascendancy.**

14:44
Our decisions play a huge role in sculpting the future, but as Dr. Wood said, the **pursuit of godly character is something that can be known.** God's will is not proven by what we achieve, but by who we are, in Him. Submission to the Heavenly Father and the course-correction it requires, are in our portfolio. We may make good decisions; we may make bad decisions; we benefit and suffer by the choices we make. But **God's will for us exists apart from the targets and accomplishments that surround us. God's will targets Himself.**

15:28
Ambition
There's a murky, outer edge to the subject of expectation. A dangerous edge.

Most of us are motivated to achieve. We are, in a word, *ambitious.* Some say, ambition is a bad thing; that at its heart, it serves the interest of self, and turns us into screaming, remorseless social climbers. Maybe this is true in some situations, and when it is, it's definitely an unflattering, soul-defeating value.

16:01
But there are some who see ambition as comprising the values that drive us to work hard, and to *be the best we can be*. There's nothing wrong with such aspiration, though you can see the potential danger. **Ambition offers a great place for pride to set up shop.** Once operational, even when it's linked to high and noble intention, ambition can be a corruptive influence.

Let's be honest. **Understanding God's will in terms of godly character can be quite unexciting.** Character is always on guard against vanity and pompous proclamation. So what's a noisy, needy, insecure personality to do? If the quiet, godly distillation of native behavior is too subtle for us, how shall we satisfy our need to achieve something notable, and be looked up to by others?

17:03
Well, one thing we could do, **we might rename our ambitious scheme, calling it** *God's will*. With that modification in place, we can then proceed to pull, hammer, and manage our way to the top because ... it's God's will, and *we have an ambition for God.*

But does God need our ambition?

17:29
Sometimes, religious leaders cross a line with their dreams. Initially, their mission has the ring of spirituality about it, so God must be on-board with the plan. They proceed to expect God's blessings on what is now *God's effort*, even though it might still be mostly, their effort. **As a tactic, such behavior is a practice of deception.** By such logic, the Crusades were launched, blanking out one of the most pivotal moments in Christ's life. If Christ rejected Peter's swordplay in the Garden of Gethsemane, by what excuse did religious Europe justify holy war?

LifePlanning Notes – Journal

18:17

Christian history is littered with good ideas that weren't necessarily God's ideas. We rename our scheme God's will, then we bang away at the subsequent challenge, **doing God a favor.** And when/if the enterprise founders, we suffer a faith-wound because God hasn't ratified our expectation and lived up to His end of our manipulated theology.

18:48
Ambition or Zeal?
Christ had plenty of opportunities for grand expectation. Influential men like Nicodemus, a religious leader, came to believe that Christ was sent from God. (John 3:1-8)

A Roman centurion acknowledged Jesus' divine authority. (Matthew 8:5-10)

A young nobleman sought Christ's counsel for how to set up a LifePlan. (Luke 18:18-23)

Just three examples, but **you have the sense, Christ fended off expectation every day.** Without hardened resolve, He could have easily dabbled in delusions-of-grandeur. He didn't, of course. And actually, **Christ's expectation was something quite different from what most of us practice.** Jesus expected death. (Mark 8:31; Mark 12:10,11; John 12:27-43)

19:58
Jesus expected death. Now there's an expectation for you. Even when people were praising Him, waving palm fronds and shouting Hosanna, Jesus expected the situation to turn against Him, ultimately. **It's safe to suggest that Christ's goal was to** do the will of ... *the one who sent me.* (John 6:39) He didn't seem to be ambitious in His own behalf, or looking for an excuse to

prove His fidelity to either Heaven, or His reputation. He probably didn't look at His calendar to see if this was the day He was scheduled beat up a few demons over in the Gadarenes, in defense of God's honor. (Matthew 8:28)

20:47
In the Temple He did beat up a few tables, where the money-changers were doing their deals, but it wasn't an act of ambition for righteous acclaim, rather, it was *zeal.* **In Psalm 69:9, Christ's behavior was anticipated several hundred years earlier:** *Zeal for thy house hath consumed me.* (see also John 2:17) There's a difference between ambition and zeal. Ambition seeks its own. Zeal for the Lord, seeks the intention of the Heavenly Father. Like Christ, we can be zealous, without risking ambition. The Heavenly Father doesn't require our insight, strength or clarity, He seeks communion and character.

21:39
What about the good side of ambition, the willingness to labor for excellence? **Perhaps the solution is** to *do all things as unto the Lord.* (Colossians 3:23) Pressing aside our schemes for advance, we are wise to develop an affection for working in a way that honors God. What could otherwise be sacrificed at the feet of pride and ambition, becomes a form of praise to our loving Creator. *Aim at Heaven and you get earth thrown in.* (Mere Christianity, C.S. Lewis)

9
DEVIL-DOG

It was an odd memory, the Devil-Dog memory. It drifted back when I decided to write a *what-if* scenario.

My wife and I have been walloped by unexpected events over the years: breast cancer, extraordinary blood pressure problems, heart murmurs, atrial fibrillation, surgery, the near-death of our only child, car accidents, financial disasters, business disasters – you'll forgive me if I don't provide more specific information, but quite honestly, I don't have the *heart* for it.

00:39

What if none of it had happened? What if we'd found a safer career-passage, early-on, and all those tests for cancer had come back, negative? What if my 10-year old son had never contracted a staff-infection? **What if life hadn't been so hard?**

00:59

Enter Abby Stage Left

The first couple of years after college, our living conditions were *newlywed-stark*. We were working for minimum-wage, trying to find our bearings and sort out our LifePlan. **Our only advantage was that we were young and in love**, and thus capable of survival at levels of misery, unthinkable today. It was into this meager world that an angel drifted in from the freeway. We named her Abby. She was one of the best dogs we would ever own: she was even-tempered, grateful and scrupulous in her practice of hygiene.

We enjoyed her company for a couple of months. Her affections lifted us past our circumstances, and in a way, she became a surrogate child. **Whatever it is that dogs do to lift your prospects, Abby did it for us. She gave us a loving point-of-focus, outside the mean little realities we faced.**

LifePlanning Notes – Journal

02:01

Then Abby chased another dog into the freeway and was hit by a car. We were standing on the curb, watching in horror when it happened. As we dragged her lifeless body to the sidewalk, I remember distinctly, the invisible words that were in my heart: *God, why did you let this happen? She's the only thing we own!* In retrospect: we didn't own her, we had claimed her. Additionally, it's interesting how the sense-of-loss attached itself rather quickly to my self-pity over our lack of owned-things. **What if Abby had dodged that car?**

02:40

After a suitable period of mourning, we scraped together every cent we could find. We bought a grief-dog, a replacement, a French Poodle puppy named Kelly. With Abby's death as the motivation, we fastened an incredible amount of affection on this fuzzy little creature. We spoiled her. Indulged her demands. Put off potty-training. We didn't want to be mean to her. By the time she was 8-months old, she'd become an adorable little terror. By the time she was 7-years old, she'd turned into a Devil-Dog.

03:18

Burrs In Our Coat

As I remembered those events from all those years ago, it hit me: we knew nothing about Abby's formative years. She entered our lives at the end of what had probably been a terrible experience of separation from her previous master. Given the burrs in her coat, we suspected that she'd been wandering for several days when she finally bumped into us.

Kelly, on the other hand, was never lost, never suffered from neglect or abuse. Her bed was always placed in the right spot, according to the season. During car rides, she was free to sit wherever she wanted, **and went into a hissy-bark if we didn't roll down the window so she could do the *nose-thing*.** She relieved herself, whenever and wherever she pleased; she growled at anyone who moved while she was eating, chewed up books and slippers, and would've done it with relish if she'd known, we had any in the refrigerator.

04:18
Kelly was not at all happy when our son was born; and in fact, with his appearance, my wife and I started ignoring her demands. By that point she was too old to engage canine-righteousness, and held a dark grudge against the baby. **We never trusted her to be alone with him.**

We've had several dogs over the years, but **Kelly was the most troublesome dog we ever owned.**

04:44
Trouble Cures
It's not convenient to point it out, but trouble, or lack thereof, may have been the distinguishing difference between Abby and Kelly. Abby had been blasted by reality. Kelly, on the other hand, had been indulged like a princess.

I hate to commend trouble, pointing out its curative effects on our lives, but you could definitely make that argument. Those who've experienced starvation tend to be incredibly thankful for the food they receive. Sudden loss of a beloved acquaintance alerts us to the special blessing of friends. Losing a good job makes us deeply appreciative of having a job, at all. Trouble **is character forming.** Even so, most of us spend a considerable amount of effort trying to avoid it, which is as it should be. **Growing character in life's garden is certainly a worthy enterprise, but you have to survive the fertilizer.**

LifePlanning Notes – Journal

05:48

Have you ever wondered: **what if there was no trouble?** What would we be like without setback or loss? **Devil-Dogs**, probably. There's another interesting twist on this phenomenon: those who've never been lost, never experience the pure relief of being found. In Luke 7:46, we hear Jesus' take on the subject. Describing the woman who'd anointed His feet with oil, Jesus pointed out ... *but whoever hasn't been forgiven much, doesn't love much.* **This is why sanctified Devil-Dogs make such incredible witnesses for Christ. They've been forgiven much.**

06:30

For the Christian, **trouble is a flash-point that alerts us to our spiritual condition, and usually provokes an audit of our LifePlan.** This is a pattern of longstanding, the practice of God's people down through the ages.

There's another implication. It might not be spiritually profitable to create an air-tight LifePlan for the future. **Assuming that we achieve easy-success with our plan, reducing our need for godly interaction, what have we won?** Flat on our backs under the basketball goal in the driveway, some of us are finally sober enough to entertain God's Fathering-technique. The complex reality may be that **trouble always finds a way, and with eternity's values in view, we may actually need it.**

07:20

It's About LifeBravery

The bottom line is an invitation to bravery. As we draft our plans, we **shouldn't be intimidated at the prospect of trouble.**

God has given us so many gifts; He's given us the gift of His Son, the Holy Spirit, and – of course – amazing grace. **His will for us is His intention for our redeemed character.** Anything the enemy throws at us has the potential for improving us. A life in communion with the Heavenly Father has wide latitude in terms of options. Whether we're 18 or 80, we should *swing for the fences*. We shouldn't be afraid of heading out for lands we don't know. With the Heavenly Father as our outfitter, **we can chase the trail with confidence.**

08:13

It might be possible to control large chunks of our LifePlan, but should that be a priority? The greatest milestone on our LifeMap should be our reliance on the Heavenly Father. **There's no way to walk the planet without bruising; and that being the case, we shouldn't be intimidated by pathways that lack the obvious targets of high prospect, money, fame, or comfort.**

> *There will be trouble*
> *Trouble will refine your life*
> *A spiritually-refined life places full confidence in God*
> *God will never leave nor forsake you (Hebrews 13:5)*

10
X-Event
Worry or Trust?

The counsel in behalf of character is probably not what most of us want to hear. Why not a little more magic? Why can't someone invent a bit of software that does all the heavy lifting? At the most, maybe the user would provide basic information like the name of their first-grade teacher or favorite color, then the program would calculate their LifePlan.

00:29
Or maybe, what about this: what about a program you could load into your GPS-unit? One that plotted your LifeMap, then calculated your next destination. Just follow the voice:

00:42
In 4-years, turn right into pre-med; stay in the left lane for 10-years; proceed to the nearest bank-teller, turn right into the deposit-lane.

Unfortunately, life doesn't organize into a predictable set of right turns. A software solution might sharpen our understanding a bit, but reality treads its own path, forward.

Here's another way to think about it. Imagine a wall representing God's will. Your vocation, then, would be like a picture nailed to that wall. The point being, when you've installed the larger, supporting frame, you have flexibility when it comes to where to hang your vocational masterpiece.

01:27
Unfortunately, some of us jump to the conclusion that if this is true, that character is what counts, then vocation doesn't matter. Which is not true. **God does care what we do; our efforts are unique; our work is worthy. It's just that, when you consider the evidence, God is always tuned to communion, character, and behavior, first.** Case-in-point: check out the list of Israel's

kings. Most of them chalked up a few accomplishments, but their crimes usually ran deeper than their contributions. **Some were rotten to the core.** King Ahab, for instance, was a good example of a really bad example. He expanded international trade by marrying a pagan princess, a sleazy, Baal-worshipping, painted hussy, prophet-killing, devil-evangelist named Jezebel. (1Kings 16) He compromised God's will by marrying this monstrosity, but the merchandising was good.

02:35

It's not what we achieve, it's who we are in the Godly context that matters. Earlier, we pointed out that Peter was a fisherman. Jesus saw this as a recommendation, but **it was Peter's reformed character that advanced his avocation.** He became the rock on whom the Lord would build His church. And if that seems like a demotion, so-be-it. Until we've subordinated our lives to the will of the Heavenly Father, like Peter, we will be denied the full reality of knowing God in His glory.

03:09

If we don't have that wall of Godly-character under construction, a LifePlan devoted to the practice of medicine may bless the community, because doctoring can be a good thing; but how disappointing for us, as we engage a LifePlan that blesses others, while denying the ultimate blessing for ourselves. What a way to waste a wall.

If you've never signed on, if you've never pursued knowing the Heavenly Father with full-intention and commitment, you're in no position to appreciate what those who have pursued Him actually experience. You'll serve your years on the planet without hearing the small click of difference that propels a Godly life into eternity. You'll rise and fall with the waves, and never be privy to the ultimate course, until the end.

04:02
Vocational Counsel
Someone suggested that most young people weren't perceptive enough to understand the importance of character; the young needed a specific suggestion like: *study for an engineering degree, or become a lawyer.*

I get the point, unfortunately. When I was 19, I couldn't even spell perceptive; I was never sure if it had one *s* or two; but not all young adults are as remedial as I turned out to be. Many do get it. They understand that **the wall of communion and character needs to be stout.** By the time we reach the end, all sorts of things will be hanging there. A poorly built wall runs the risk of collapsing, before – if not after – our last breath.

04:48
Fortunately, wherever we are on the LifeMap, when we finally reach a level of understanding, we can reorder our perspective without a lot of penalty. Our **faulty perceptions in the beginning don't have to be permanent.** In an instant, we can switch to God's will by simply **recalibrating our LifePlan with eternity's values in view.** This was pretty much what happened with the thief on the cross. The distance between being out of God's will and stepping into God's will is probably a couple of seconds. Maybe less.

Godly character answers the question: *How shall we proceed into the future?* **It also resolves the larger issue:** *How shall we proceed into eternity?*

05:36
Where To Start?
And how should we proceed? What's the bottom line?

LifePlanning Notes – Journal

In a word, we should start our quest, **prayerfully**. Many people see prayer as purely ceremonial. It's not. As you linger over the future, prayerfully engaged, God often reveals His most splendid secrets about the future. *You should bathe your efforts in prayer.* In Dr. Wood's message, the word bathed suggested an *immersive act of Godly communion,* which is a fairly compelling thought.

06:10
How long should you pray about your vocation? How will you know for sure what God is trying to tell you?

These questions are resolved within the communion-space you share with the Heavenly Father. And let's not be too understated about this. **God never suspends your freedoms, disengaging your need for faith.** God's will is that all come into communion with Him. As a result, getting bent-out-of shape over how to guess our way forward, is a bit pathetic.

06:42
What To Expect
When you finally set a course, what happens next? How do you find your niche?

Actually, the first big pattern suggests that you really never arrive at a niche, but spend most of your life, **swinging, niche-to-niche. Vocational progress is marked by climbing, stretching, falling, recovering, and restarting.** A lot like mountain climbing: *niche-to -niche; handhold to handhold; band-aid to band-aid.*

07:15
Zeroing In On Launch
If you have a strong sense of what you're supposed to do, **that's**

where you start. If not, do you have special interests, or capabilities that suggest a vocational direction? Only you know that answer. But remember, your skills and curiosities are gifts from God. **It's possible that the arrows pointing to the future will launch from one of these** *gifts-of-interest.*

Have you had a special revelation, a dream or a vision that suggests a particular course? Perhaps your sense-of-purpose targets a special burden you can't shake, or maybe a heightened awareness of something, someone needs to do. Why not you?

08:02
God beckons us to the future in so many ways. Even so, we shouldn't get too worked up over the missed bulls-eyes. **Life doesn't boil down to perfect scores or getting** ducks in a row.

Prayerfully, as you puzzle your way forward, **what are the obvious possibilities?**

Chances are fairly good that someone has already covered the ground you plan to travel. Spend a bit of effort. Find out what those who've gone before had to say. **Experience is not always the best teacher; someone else's experience is even better.**

08:33
Restarting
The subject of LifePlanning is a natural discussion for the young, but **it's also an issue in the lives of those of us who are older.** Most seniors have already visited square one, even when we can't quite remember when or where it was. If we've lived long enough, we've seen the evidence:

> *Extra effort isn't always rewarded*
> *The threat of blackmail is far more respected than the*

LifePlanning Notes – Journal

09:10
Most seniors have experienced these nasty little realities, first-hand. Still, against all this survival-wisdom, many of us find ourselves in the sad position of restarting at 30, 40, 50 ... 60 ... 70.

Restarts for a senior can be devastating, and the subject is so massive, it falls outside the design of this presentation. It deserves its own special course-ware.

09:42
There are some important observations, though. First, anyone who's been in the job-market understands the notion of swinging, niche-to-niche. Looking back, it's fascinating to remember all the different transactions, good and bad, that mark our employment experience. When you're 50, and get laid off, in the coarsest possible terms: **you've merely arrived at another handhold, another band-aid.** You've survived them in the past, you'll survive them in the future.

10:12
What's most troubling, though, is the sense that we've failed, that we didn't play the game well, or were judged, *incapable*, or *unworthy*. On examination, those perspectives are usually way-off-the-mark. If we were worthy enough, going into our last employment niche, chances are fairly good that we were advanced based on evidence. **Most of us are kicked to the curb for reasons, outside our vantage point.** There's usually a specific component, like the one mentioned before. The big boss' son-in-law needed a job – your job. It's usually nothing personal, just business. **You are easily replaced.**

10:52
Quick Counsel For Re-starters
Proceed from where you are. If you're no longer 14-years old, don't assume that you've got to head over to the neighbor's house with a borrowed lawnmower and a gallon of gas. **Your accrued skills are worth something, to someone.** When your emotional state settles, your first job is *finding that someone.* **Let your wisdom-of-years inform the diligence of your search.**

The first reasonable course-of-action involves *bathing the situation in prayer.* Chances are, the Heavenly Father will open your eyes to new opportunities. **Perhaps He'll bring to mind an earlier course-of-action that is now close-by.**

11:56
Many seniors who've been dumped prematurely, find quick interest from those companies that used to be the competition. Ethics require you to protect your old company, in terms of trade secrets, but you have a right to work. And typically, the courts will agree. Check the competition when you restart.

Who knows? Ready or not, **maybe it's time to retire.** If so, your new chapter in life should begin as all the others: *bathed in prayer.*

12:09
My Grandfather's Retirement
My grandfather was a rural pastor. In the early 1900s, small country churches didn't pay much, so my grandfather earned a living, farming.

By modern standards, he endured an exhausting life. When my grandparents reached their 70s, **grandpa was physically worn** out, and grandma could no longer take care of him.

12:33
I was only 9-years old at the time, so while I saw the drama unfold from the periphery, I came to understand **the tough reality that comes with aging, strangely,** as I grew older.

Grandpa was a bit of an antique by the end. When the church he had pioneered needed a younger minister, grandfather stepped aside, but he was deeply bruised by the transition. The discovery that **you're not wanted because you're too old, is one of life's most devastating moments.** And you don't necessarily get a lot of sympathy.

13:07
When he was finally incapacitated to the point, he was crawling, room-to-room, in that remote little west Texas farmhouse, **grandpa's disengagement with his LifePlan was complete.**

On a rainy afternoon, our family hopped into the car and headed out to west Texas for an emergency intervention. Grandma and grandpa would have to leave the farm.

I sat in the front seat between my father and grandfather, on the three hour journey back home. I remember the huge raindrops on the windshield. I remember the strange silence, the muffled tears from my exhausted grandmother, in the back-seat, where she was sitting with my mom and my brother.

13:51
Over the next few months, grandpa gave up. Lost his appetite. Finally, my dad took him to the doctor, to check for any underlying issues. They found nothing. Nothing, except the deadly reality of a restart.

Grandpa explained the obvious. **He had become unnecessary;** he worried that he'd made mistakes with his life; **he saw no place where he could be of any use to anyone;** he said, *there were still so many people, walled off to the reality of Christ's resurrection, and what it meant to them.*

The doctor finally had heard enough. He squared off with my grandfather, looked him in the eyes and told him what he needed to hear.

14:29
Do you have any grandchildren?

Well, of course he did. Grandpa was living with two incredible grandchildren at the moment, and there were several incredible cousins strung out across the continental US. The plan was that he and grandma would have a chance to live with them all, in the months ahead.

So, you've got a new job, Reverend Wray. Grandchildren.

14:52
The suggestion must have brought pause to grandpa, but he replied: *What about the people I never reached?*

I've no idea whether or not the doctor measured his words. He looked gramps in the eye and said: *Reverend Wray, you're going to have to let the rest of them just go to Hell.*

Let me stop right there. Since you probably never my grandpa, you have no idea how this would've fallen on his ears. In younger days, he would've been unleashed by such words, and risen like a dragon of godliness and denounced such hellish counsel. But this time, he didn't. Because **in a way, the doctor was preaching from the Bible, and gramps had to listen.**

15:35
Sometimes, after you serve your generation well, you fall on sleep. And if you're not quite asleep yet, you exhaust what remains of the day with your grandchildren.

Those kids are your new mission, Reverend Wray. It's time to let someone else take up the other one. You're not finished. You've just got a new job.

Grandpa lived the rest of his days without a formal pulpit, but he lived as a tender, loving, amazing example of Godly character. His tenderness and wisdom were in full bloom. And for the first time, his grandchildren had a chance **to take a second look – a closer look – at a LifePlan, well-lived.**

Restarting is the opportunity for discovery, and a chance to fall-up.

16:25
The Way It Works
More than I care to admit, I've blamed God for the bad things that have happened. Seldom do I hold a grudge against the enemy of my soul, preferring instead, to blame its champion.

Unfortunately, evil exists. **There's a dark intelligence to it, and conspiracy in its method.** Even more unfortunate, the enemy's subversion of our LifePlan usually travels the most unlikely trail of all: **self-pity.** Lined up on either side of our LifeTrail are our grievances, both real and imagined; **self-justification is there, as well as self-compensation, and self-indulgence. Satan snares us, employing all sorts of emotionally-based mechanisms that**

show up in the absence of character's discretion.

17:17
And then, when Satan achieves a moment of devastation, in the zone where we've quarantined God's will, what do we do? We blame God.

Why don't we blame Satan for his felonious assaults? By his efforts we are dismissed, bruised – to the level of the soul – laid waste by sudden blood and slow-fading; **his dark arts aim at breaking us, goading us into cursing God, then dying.** And many of us do just that.

Perhaps we should remember: Christ was crucified. **If evil can attach itself to Heaven's plan-of-salvation, then we shouldn't be surprised when it chases us to ground, as well.**

18:01
What Is God's Defense?
Why doesn't God get the praise when, **by the end, our lives bloom at every place where there's been pruning?** Think about it this way. When we've pursued the nurturing of Godly character, then we get hit with a scalding blow, we might actually die. Which would slip us into the loving presence of the Lord.

Most who've passed along that brink in a near death experience, don't want to leave. But then, the other option is, maybe we won't die, but flourish like a rose bush at the point of the wound. Either way, whether liberated to ultimate peace, in God's direct presence, or transformed, in life into a more spectacular and aromatic faith, **the enemy's dark magic is unwound.**

18:50
There's a great account in the Old Testament involving Sam-

son, the strong man who killed a lion. As Samson passed by daily, as the carcass wasted in the sun, a nest of bees took up residence in the decaying remains. (Judges 14:8) It's a mildly gross image, but it's powerful. Samson was also intrigued by the contrast. And this just about sums up the way God works with our LifePlan. After subduing a predator-force, the point-of-attack becomes the province of sweet surprise.

19:24
Unintended Consequence – The Godly Sort
When you think back to the worst things in your life, when you were assaulted, when you lost your life savings, when you were accused, unfairly, don't you also see sparkles of God's compensation? No, the bruise may remain, and the loss, never compensated, but aren't there small surprises that mark the trail, outbound from the lions you survive? And that's God's contribution. Salvation. Blessing. Sweet from bitter. Light from dark.

20:03
Even when the Enemy aims a dark hammer at our LifePlan, that hammer marks the spot where there will be honey. Perhaps you'll live the rest of your life alone, or survive in the shadows of poverty, but God will astonish you with the way He re-manufactures pain into blessing and communion. When our LifePlan aims at Heaven, our passage on Earth passes from glory-to-glory. Because our Lord has said: *I will never leave you nor forsake you.* And when our lives are cast into alignment with His, our LifePlan is sure, and true ... and ultimate.

- End -

Appendices

Surviving the Rapture

So, how did you get here, to this point-in-time? More importantly, how will your proceed … from here?

Will you use the same old mind-tools you've used in the past and proceed to jump from one hole into a deeper hole? That's for you to decide.

Sooner-or-later, there's going to be an evacuation, a planetary evacuation, where an entire layer of human culture will be suddenly and quietly removed. But if the extraction is a quiet event, what follows will be apocalyptic. Almost immediately, everyone will be trying to unpack what happened, and one of the first explanations will be that it was actually the Rapture. Where Christian believers were abruptly taken into the presence of the Jesus Christ. It's a prophecy of long-standing.

The trouble is, a lot of people who identified themselves as Christians will still be here, and to complicate things a bit, quite a few people who weren't Christians, and even went so far as to be publicly anti-Christian, will have disappeared. Anyone looking for a simple explanation is going to have a problem.

But the real trouble is: you're still here. And now, you have to make a choice. Because what just happened is the key to what happens next, and this is where you really need to be using new mind tools.

So, if it was the Rapture, the Bible contains all the information needed to explain what happens next, and what you need to do to fix the condition of your life. But what if an alternative explanation has its own appeal. It will most likely be something along the lines of:

The time has come for full disclosure. There are life forms from beyond the earth; there are lifeforms living deep within the earth.
In the beginning, our non-terrestrial brothers and sisters wanted us to find the way on our own, but they've been increasingly worried about our weapons, our lousy choice of leaders, and the way we've been destroying the planet. And one of their greatest concerns: there are too many humans. Earth can't sustain our population.

Given the choice between letting us starve to death, or finding an inhumane relief through warfare, their solution was to use technology to extract, then graft a portion of earth's population into a new planetary system, somewhere else.

Which might sound plausible. So, was it the Rapture? If so, that's religion. Or was it an alien mercy? If so, that's science fiction.

How do you choose? There will be many convincing proofs that will seem to authenticate a particular point-of-view, but there's one you should be paying serious attention to. If you are looking for testimonial proof for the Rapture, the voices most profoundly capable of advancing that declaration … are gone. Their robust evidence for a Jesus-event can't be argued because their voices are silent. And that should tell you something big.

Perhaps that's the greatest proof of all. Their absence gives the

LifePlanning Notes - Journal

strongest possible voice for what happened and what path you should take next Jesus event.

Love & Evil

The Bible says that God created the cosmos. If so, did He also create evil?

We see God's signature everywhere. In the recursive patterning of the universe we see a unity-of-process. Our solar system, for example, is structured atop the same pattern we also see in atomic structure. A large body, orbited by smaller bodies.

Another question. Why did God create us? What did He need that He didn't already have?

The Bible doesn't tell us everything, but it tells us everything we need to know, the most important being that we were created. Made in the image of God. This is interesting because God reveals Himself as a father in Holy Scripture.

In the book of Genesis, God observed that it wasn't good for man to be alone. At the other end of the cosmos, maybe it wasn't good for God to be alone, either. If the pattern of fatherhood tells us anything, it suggests the powerful, deep affection we fathers hold for our children. The same would be true — in a far grander sense —for God, as well. And this confronts us with another created thing. Freedom.

God designed the pattern of freedom into the things He made, and He exalts in affection freely given. But Freedom to love also means freedom NOT to love.

This is the origin of evil. If God had not invested freedom … there would not be the freedom to choose evil, but there wouldn't be love, either. As strange as it may seem, love and evil are rooted in freedom.

According to the Bible, there are other life-forms in the cosmos, and some of them used their freedom to exalt themselves as gods. This marks the precise spot where the war between good and evil is waged. Which is a stupid war, when you think about it. Because God cannot be defeated. But maybe that's not the point. What if God can be wounded?

As the wannabe gods peel away the free affections of God's little blind tribe of humanity, perhaps they are calculating that these little lost souls are so beloved by the Heavenly Father, their rejection of Him brings little blind woundings to God's love.

What could possibly be the endgame in this?

God's anguish over the spoiling of the human soul is the only weapon they have against Him. And now, the dark judgment for all wannabe gods is about to be handed down. That's what the Rapture was all about. God removed His community of believers to preserve them from what happens next. If there is a silver lining here, this gives you more time to end your war with God. It won't be easy, but it is doable. And the Bible pre-celebrates your victory as a Tribulation saint.

What do you have to do? Well, what all of us have done. Jesus said: "No man comes to the Father except through me." So ask Jesus to connect you to the Heavenly Father, ask Him forgive your sins. Acknowledge Him as your Savior. And that's it. That's the threshold. Find a Bible. Study Jesus' life and His words. Pray. Let your mind be renewed by the Holy Spirit.

Holding true to a new life won't be easy, but we are waiting for you on the other side, and rooting for you. God is too. He has not abandoned you. Draw near to God and He will draw near to you. Taste and see that the Lord is good. Choose wisely. Choose now.

Next

The Bible tells you everything you need to know about fixing your life.

Start by reading about Jesus. There are other biblical characters, of course, but all narratives — in one way or other — point to His appearance 2,000 years ago. Whether the subject is the sacrifice for sin, the kingship of David, the exile of Israel, or the prophecies of Daniel and Isaiah, the weight of scripture is oriented to Christ.

So read about His earthly existence in the books of Matthew, Mark, Luke and John. Jesus healed people. Brought the dead back to life. Through parable and direct statement, Jesus described the nature of the cosmos and His relationship with the Heavenly Father.

C.S. Lewis observed that you can't call Jesus just a great teacher. Though He was that. Given His power over nature, disease and death, He was either crazy, or who He said He was: the Son of God on a mission to take away the sins of the world.

So read about Jesus. Then accept or reject Him as your Lord and Savior. It's your choice, and that's what you do next. Choose.

Like the rest of us, though, after reading you'll probably find yourself hopelessly drawn to Christ. That's is as it should be.

Jesus once said: "If you love me, keep my commandments." Ok. Then this is what you do next. Read the standards that Jesus established in the Sermon on the Mount. Recast your life across the patterns of behavior you discover there.

Finally, the last thing that Jesus said before He ascended into

Heaven was a commandment to seek empowerment from on high. The book of Acts goes into great detail about this power. As your life is being reformed through scripture and prayer, be filled with the Spirit, because you need God's power for the challenges you now face.

And what about those challenges? They are now looming big-time in your life.

What happens next? God will never leave you or forsake you. Aou don't have to power-thru on your own strength. God's power will sustain you as you make your way to your eternal destiny, where we hope to see you ... soon.

Get Over It

Discouragement and despair are two things that you can't afford. Yesterday's community of Christian believers are no longer available, but the gift of salvation is still yours to claim.

Acknowledge Christ as Savior. Meditate on Holy Scripture. Commune with God through prayer. Take deep root in God's provision because you face tough times. And holding true, or as Scripture puts it, "enduring to the end," is the only real challenge you have at the moment.

There is a strong possibility you will face a competitive theology. A god-belief that is in opposition to THE true God-belief. You have to discern which is which.

In his book *Dimensions*, Dr. Jacques Vallée made the point that if you took a wide view of UFO phenomena, trying to find some kind of perspective on the lights zipping around the sky, or cosmic visitations, or the mad, a la carte messages from our space brothers — it might turn out that there is something else, something beyond a direct explanation. Someone, or some force in the universe might be running a psychological operation, attempting to influence human belief through conditioned response.

And now, openly, UFO-theology offers a competitive view of origins and destines.

Competitive with what? Well, draw a line from Jesus Christ. Draw it backwards in time to the beginning of recorded history. God revealed Himself along this path. And UFO-theology is competitive with that.

LifePlanning Notes – Journal

According to UFO-history, "people from other planets" assisted with the development of Nazi weapons during World War II. (Herman Oberth). A war that claimed at least 50-million human lives. Why would our ET brothers, given their professed interest in peace and harmony, why would they provide weapons-technology to Nazi Germany? And when those Nazi programs were grafted into the US military, why did our space brothers continue providing technical know-how for the military? Put another way, beyond the cheap moralizing, why do they talk peace, but trade in blood toys? Why didn't they, also step from behind the curtain and introduce themselves? Why didn't they go head-to-head with Jesus Christ the Messiah and establish their own path from one end of history to the other? The answer is, because they couldn't.

Is the Rapture a misreading of an ET event? Or is the ET explanation a misrepresentation of a Jesus-Promise? One path deals in origins and destinies and has a track record. The other doesn't.

There is a big difference. The ET story ends in myth. The God story just led to the Rapture of the church.

Choose between them and choose wisely. Your eternity hangs in the balance.

———————

Production Note
Surviving the Rapture is a test scribe, focused on one of the controversial teachings of the church. Given that so many events "pre-described" in Scripture are becoming reality, it seemed, a worthy test. It was initially imagined as presenting more patterns

LifePlanning Notes – Journal

and biblical citations regarding the prophecy.

Production took place in 2015-16.

HOLYbook

The HOLYbook for Christians is divided into two parts.

The first, the Old Testament, is the foundation on which the second, the New Testament is constructed. That's how they're linked. The Old set the stage for the New.

In terms of content, the New Testament focuses on the life and teachings of Jesus Christ, who lived approximately 2,000 years ago. The historical record of Jesus is drawn from an astonishingly short, 3-year period of time. What Jesus said, what He did over those three years, that's the heart and soul of the New Testament.

The Old Testament go back much further than the time of Christ, and originated in the special relationship between God, the Creator, and the family into which Jesus would eventually be born. The Old Testament was written between the 14th and 5th centuries BCE, a stretch of time covering roughly 900-years.

Approximately 30 writers authored the narrative of the Old Testament, but the writings started started with one man. Moses. Raised in the Egyptian palace, he was educated as a member of the royal family, but Moses was also a Jew. He not only had access to the libraries of Egypt. He also had access to the spoken

LifePlanning Notes – Journal

accounts of Jewish oral tradition.

Now, jump back ahead a thousand years or so. The New Testament was written in the first century A.D. by people who were with Jesus during the three years of His public ministry, were with … or had direct access to first-hand evidence.

This turns into a big issue when discussing the origin of the New Testament. It contains eyewitness accounts to the miracles and teachings of Jesus, as well as the letters that circulated among the first Christian communities.

Jesus Christ, the Son of God, was raised from the dead. He was seen alive by people who had also seen His death. And the dead don't come back. Resurrection authenticated His divine authority, because regular humans don't come back from the dead, and regular humans don't reshape planetary history based on three years of public behavior.

Protected Narrative

In the beginning was the word, and the word was published … mouth-to-mouth. People drew their histories and instruction from oral narrative, and then memorized these narratives, carefully.

Here's the advantage to oral tradition. When you don't understand something a speaker says, you can interrupt them directly, and ask for clarification. Something you can't do directly with the author of a written page. And if the speaker says something that's not true, you can correct the untruth, publicly, in the same airspace where it was told. It's called "peer review," and it's still fundamental to both the spoken word and written scholarship. If you lie, whatever the narrative source, you get ratted out.

At the time of Jesus, oral tradition was still an active part the culture. In fact, peer review exerted a strong influence on His biographies. (Matthew, Mark Luke, and John, the first four books in the New Testament)

What if, way back in the first century … someone decided to jazz up the Jesus-history, adding a bit of fiction … say … Jesus has a snowball fight with a couple of Abominable Snowmen. What would've been the result?

Peer reviewers in the first century, people who knew the Jesus account directly, would've screamed bloody murder.

There's a good reason for making this point.

How we got the Bible, why some books were included and others weren't, these are issues framed by scholarship and provenance.

LifePlanning Notes – Journal

The Bible contains written snapshots of the important God-moments in human culture, carefully curated by those who sought to protect the narrative as an act of truth-keeping. That's the point. God's Word has been carefully guarded.

In terms of protected narrative, no book in history even comes close.

The Bible traveled to us across thousands of years, through countless languages and forgotten cultures. It was held in high esteem, protected by scholarship and a hard allegiance to the original language. It's an amazing document.

How The Bible Found Its Words

Most of us don't know how we got the Bible. One myth is that it was written by a bunch of old, dead, white guys. Wrong.

Another is: the Bible just fell from the sky.
Well, figuratively speaking, maybe you could say it like that, but specifically speaking, wrong again. The words in the Bible originated in God's covenant with a human family.

A covenant is an agreement, like a contract. For your obedience to my commandments, through your descendants all of the nations of the world will be blessed.
The voice of God is heard in dreams and visions, or directly, as described in the cases of Abraham, Samuel, John-the-Baptist, or Saint Paul. But the voice of the Lord is also heard within the inner narrative that everyone experiences. David, the king of Israel, referred to it.

In our culture, the prospect is usually dismissed as delusional. So most of us have been detuned when it comes to hearing God.
We are often unaware of His voice. God has given us the freedom to listen, or not, or listen at low volume. If you are tune in, though; if you're reading the Bible, or in a worship service, you may notice thoughts that just show up, apart from your contemplative processes. Certainly not all voices are God's, but learning to distinguish God's voice is one of the disciplines of faith and the practice of ultimate perception. The person who seeks God will find him. The person who doesn't seek, doesn't find. Simple as that. I's a choice.

LifePlanning Notes – Journal

A non-God seeker might say, see you're tricking yourself. You think you're seeing God, but you're seeing what you want to see.

This logic cuts to ways. A God-seeker could, say you don't think you're seeing God, but you're not seeing what you don't want to see. *Draw near to God, and He will draw near to you.* Since the beginning, people have passionately drawn near, and God has chosen them for communion.

It is at the heart of this communion, the Bible found its words.

Production Note

HOLYbook is a test scribe, focused on the core document in Christianity. The Holy Bible. The drafting outline anticipated a far grander project than personal resources allowed. The unforunate loss of the covenant, as a scribe, is a glaring hole in this brief pre-sentation. Covenant is the premise from which Christ's salvation emerges.

Production took place in 2017-2018.

Reactions

"Scribe-Geezer is unexpected. Took time to adjust to the multiple media approach. Definitely NOT your father's paperback, but it's probably the future of books. Using the QR-code was simple, which is especially important for a non-techie. (me)"

"The content is sophisticated but approachable. And not just as course-ware for young adults. The folks who taught the book to the high school class were as hooked as the students. We heard a lot of laughing. If that means anything."

"It was 'a trip to a land I did not know.' Here's what I figured out. First, watch the scribes (animations) on a tablet (or phone). Then read. And if you're bent accordingly, watch, read, and listen at the same time. Whatever. But be prepared. When it finally comes together in your head, it's big. Christianity, powerfully sorted."

"Fantastic. Insightful Christian themes, seldom discussed. The book goes to a lot of unexpected places. For instance, I'd never thought about Jesus as a baby, and how aware he might have been in the manger. I'll never read the Christmas story again without thinking about what baby Jesus might have been thinking: 'Cue the shepherds.'"

"I love books. Reading is vital for your head. It's interesting to read a 'written book', empowered - not diminished - by media. Who knew?"

"I can see this as a powerful tool for young Christian believers. Takes you the the heart of the 'elephant in the room.' What are you going to be when you grow up?"

"As an 'elderly' person – I think that's what they call us – I saw things I'd never realized before. Wishing that I'd seen this earlier in life is something on the order of an understatement. Better late than never."